Advance Praise for *Shap*

"Every college student studies under the influ
to be that influence. With two college-bound kids of my own, I would give this
book to anyone who would have the courage to help shape their future."

Tim Hawkins
Director of Sojourn Collegiate Ministries
Chaplain at MIT

"There's no shortage of talking heads opining on the failures of today's young
adults. The problem is many of them don't work with young adults. They're
observers, not participants. Dr. Guy Chmieleski is a refreshing exception.
He's an academic and a practitioner who has devoted his life to working with
college students. He has earned the right to be heard. And what he has to say is
wise, practical, and hope filled. *Shaping Their Future* is an indispensable guide
for anyone who cares about the next generation. The book is crammed with
wisdom on how to help young people navigate the rocky terrain of early adulthood while growing in their commitment to follow Jesus. I'll be recommending
Shaping Their Future to anyone with a heart for young people."

Drew Dyck
Managing Editor of *Leadership Journal*
Author of *Generation Ex-Christian*

"Guy Chmieleski has provided a welcome guide in a time when mentoring
relationships are more important than ever! This book is great for campus
ministers, pastors of college congregations, and other mentors who work with
college students. Guy draws from the best scholarship related to the changing
needs of emerging adults as well as his own personal and ministry experiences.
He identifies the central role of mentoring relationships in the faith development of young adults and is spot-on in describing the changing relational skills
of college students. The chapter topics are relevant and clear, the 'Mentor's
Toolbox' provides excellent applications, and he gives handles for those seeking
to navigate a mentoring relationship. It is a great resource for both experienced
guides and those who are only beginning to be a positive presence in the life of
young adults."

Rev. Ashlee Alley
Director of Campus Ministry
Southwestern College, Winfield, Kansas

"The thesis of this book is straightforward and true: College students are
traversing the exciting, risky, and often dangerous path to adulthood. They
need mentors who know what they're getting into and will give themselves
to formative relationships with college students. Written by an attentive and
insightful practitioner, this book is wise, savvy, honest, and real. Each chapter
starts with where we are and leads to where we need to go. It weaves personal
experience with pastoral reflection. The 'Mentor's Toolbox' asks probing

questions that keep us on track. Guy mentors us as he teaches how to mentor others. I heartily recommend this book."

Rev. Dr. Stephen Rankin
Chaplain and Minister to the University at Southern Methodist University
Author of *Aiming at Maturity: The Goal of the Christian Life*

"*Shaping the Future* by Dr. Guy Chmieleski is an excellent book for campus ministers, professors, parents, pastors, and university officials—anyone who is concerned about the future of today's collegians and the young "emerging" adult population. These collegians are in the transition of a lifetime! The reader will find how crucial our role is in helping today's young generation navigate healthy autonomy, relationships, and purpose. Chmieleski draws from his own personal experience as a college student and his research and years of serving on campus and provides practical ways we can lead, influence, and resource this future generation through intentional mentoring relationships."

Dennis Gaylor
National Director of Chi Alpha Campus Ministries, USA
Springfield, Missouri

"Too often we only hear about how college students aren't where we think they should be, which simply is not mutually beneficial to the body of Christ. Thankfully, Guy doesn't allow us to arrogantly posture ourselves in shallow misunderstanding but instead brings practical insights to the core issues needing to be addressed and does so in a way that gently nudges us toward intentionally making disciples from a heart that is motivated by love."

Chuck Bomar
Pastor of Colossae Church, Portland, Oregon
Founder of CollegeLeader (CollegeLeader.org)
Author of *Better Off Without Jesus* and
Worlds Apart: Understanding the Mindset and Values of 18–25 Year Olds

"If there is any doubt that today's college students are in need of wise and compassionate mentors, Guy Chmieleski's book expertly dispels it. He writes from fifteen years of experience, giving us convincing evidence as well as helpful resources to do the job. This book is an essential tool for those of us who are willing to accept the call to mentor a generation that waits for us to lead the way."

Tracy Balzer
Director of Christian Formation at John Brown University
Author of *A Listening Life*

"Every college student needs a mentor, and every mentor needs this book."

Tyler Ellis
College Minister at the University of Delaware
Author of *Question Everything*

"The college years have the potential to be one of the most life-shaping seasons of one's life, but the determining factor is how well students continue to grow and mature in that new setting. In *Shaping Their Future*, Guy Chmieleski helps potential mentors understand a big-picture approach to how to relate and guide college students so that they can navigate through the transition and into a healthy life in college."

Tommy McGregor
Founder of TheTransMission
Author of *Lost in Transition: Becoming Spiritually Prepared for College*

"There is a crisis of faith and maturity among today's college and university students. One of *the* best answers to this crisis is mature, adult mentors who will listen and speak loving truth in their lives. Guy Chmieleski's book, *Shaping Their Future*, gives you an insight into what the students are going through, but more importantly he helps you understand their thought process. At the end of each section is the "Mentor's Toolbox," which you will find to be a wonderful and practical help in your walking with students. Whether you are a professional college minister or a layperson who cares, you will find this book everyday helpful!"

Arliss Dickerson
Leadership Development Consultant for Baptist Collegiate Ministry

"In *Shaping Their Future*, Guy Chmieleski identifies the key developmental areas experienced by college students. Based on his own experiences as a student and now as a spiritual mentor, Chmieleski offers practical guidance for making intentional interventions in the lives of the students we encounter. Acknowledging that the college years are crucial to the growth of students, he encourages us as mentors to go beyond superficial relationships and to challenge students to dig deeper so greater strides are made as students prepare for a life that makes a difference in their world for Jesus Christ."

Dr. Joe Brockinton
Vice President for Student Life at Southern Wesleyan University

"Guy has broken this topic down into bite-size chunks that are simple with relevant themes important in any mentoring relationship. I found myself reflecting not only on my position in higher ed and opportunity to mentor but on my parenting too.

"*Shaping Their Future* is a great call to take the initiative carefully but *take the initiative* in mentoring and challenging students in our spheres of influence to grow spiritually in healthy ways. Thanks for putting this out there!

"As a higher education administrator for twenty-five years and father of three adult college students, I loved the opportunity to interact with topics that are incredibly relevant in shaping the next generation of leaders. This is a book that a wide variety of people will resonate with."

Dr. Mark Troyer
Vice President for Enrollment Management at Asbury University

"Life with God is an adventure. For many the university years are a defining part of that adventure. Through humor and fresh insight, Guy Chmieleski does a masterful job in creating for us a practical blueprint on how to best prepare this generation for the full experience."

Dave Short
National Director of Campus Alpha, Alpha USA

"Shaping their Future is a must read for anyone seeking to mentor college students, point them to Jesus, and prepare them for the rest of their lives. Students need and want your help! This is your field manual that not only gives you great insight to many of the most critical topics they wrestle with, but also helps you ask life-changing questions and journey with them more effectively."

John Allert
Executive Director of Campus Ministry Toolbox

"As willing as our hearts are to pour into college students, the responsibility that we have as mentors to the younger generation can often be daunting. Guy Chmieleski doesn't sugarcoat the challenges that we face in coming alongside college students today, but he does offer encouragement and insight that will help us in the process. Chmieleski provides us with an in-depth understanding of college students—their faith and worldview, their understanding of college, money, responsibility, freedom, intimacy, and their place in the world. Understanding their value systems, families of origin, and how culture has shaped them equips us to engage with them in a meaningful way—a way that invites them into a journey of pursuing God's truth, gaining meaningful experiences, claiming more responsibility, and asking tough questions.

"This book is a helpful tool in preparing us to pursue meaningful relationships with this generation of college students in order to help them make the most of their formative college years. Chmieleski challenges us to stop waiting for opportunities to develop these relationships and be intentional with initiating and building them—our students are counting on us too! His sense of urgency in this is one that resonates—we are doing students a disservice by allowing them to waste such a significant season of their lives; college can be a time of squandering opportunities and wandering aimlessly, or it can be one of incredible growth and formation. Chmieleski's invitation for us to invest in this generation is one we must take seriously, and his book is a useful guide into investing in their growth and development in a way that is life giving and guided by the transforming powers of the Holy Spirit."

Brad Baker
Pastor to College Students at Saddleback Church

"Dr. Guy Chmieleski has written an insightful and informative book that will assist anyone working with young adults in making the very most out their formative years. Read this book with a pen, paper, and a highlighter at the ready! There is much to glean and immediately apply from this book. It is a much-needed resource for a pivotal season of life."

Pastor Laurel Bunker
Dean of Campus Ministries
Campus Pastor at Bethel University

Shaping Their Future

Mentoring Students Through
Their Formative College Years

Dr. Guy Chmieleski

seedbed PUBLISHING

Printed in the United States of America

Print ISBN: 978-1-62824-026-9
Mobipocket ISBN: 978-1-62824-027-6
ePub ISBN: 978-1-62824-028-3
uPDF ISBN: 978-1-62824-029-0

Library of Congress Control Number: 2013932276

Cover design by Abe Goolsby – officinaabrahae.com
Interior design by Lisa Parnell – lparnell.com

SEEDBED PUBLISHING
Sowing for a Great Awakening
204 N. Lexington Avenue, Wilmore, Kentucky 40390
www.seedbed.com

*Few and far between are teens
whose lives are shaped by purpose,
who demonstrate direction,
who recognize their interdependence
with communities small and large,
or who think about what it means to live
in the biggest house in the global village.*

—

Tim Clydesdale,
The First Year Out

Contents

Foreword

Shaping. Forming. Crafting a life.

Jesus did most of His work in ordinary places with ordinary people—in the streets, on the road, in homes, over meals—as He lived life "on the way to the next thing." We learn from Him there are no walls to the places or the people who can teach us to know God. Some are occasional, seemingly coincidental moments or people who touch our lives and shape us simply by proximity. But some are those with whom we linger over life as friends in conversation over good coffee. Mentors have other names and roles in students' lives: coaches, faculty, supervisors, pastors, advisors, RAs, etc. They form relationships in which they choose to be present to students for their formation.

My relationship with Guy Chmieleski is one of those for me. Our friendship most often took place in college cafeterias, the campus ministry office, and coffee shop tables. He was a student; I was his campus pastor. He was willing to speak his mind with big questions and sometimes to listen. We got on well and continue as friends to this day. I no longer know who the mentor is, but I know we learned how to meet at the intersections where life is lived authentically—in questions, occasional answers, pain and failure, success and joy—in decisions needing to be settled and choices to be made. Shaping, forming, and crafting life took place in those conversations.

Such a relationship is not only for a few but is something necessary for each of us. Eugene Peterson said it best: "I am not myself by myself." A person's development depends on continuous exposure to other people who themselves embody identity, formation, and vision.

We should know it by now: we do not come to faith alone. We are not *self-made* but inherently *other-made* by those precious ones who shape and form and craft us by their words, questions, prayers, and time. We should know it by now: we need the wisdom of others to help us find our own. Mentoring is a gift that continually gives to each. The role of mentors is not that of a professional theologian or spiritual expert but rather one with the willingness to do the hard work of listening to the story God is writing in the days and nights of the other. It doesn't require specialized certification as much as it requires a curiosity and willingness for deep enough listening and deep enough seeing into the shaping work of that Artist who is crafting a life. We should know it by now: we all need someone to tell our stories to. We are formed and shaped and crafted for life by the mysterious power of questions and words. We live into our stories as we tell them to others willing to listen.

Spiritual mentoring is something we all need and all can give. The requisite skill is fairly simple: it's like taking a walk with one of my young grandsons. You know how that goes: It doesn't usually take us in a straight line. We stop and wonder and look and talk. We repeat words and go back and look again. We meander and wander. We look and look, and always there is wonder about something larger than just us—it might be a butterfly or bird or penny on the street.

Mentoring is a holy invitation to enter life with another in just that way—to participate in Jesus' story as we walk our way through life. There is always the danger we will get sidetracked and think the story is only about us—that's why we need others to help shape the conversations and set the table with the food of the gospel. We aren't the Artist shaping and molding and crafting as if we know the ultimate shape of the other, but we walk with the Artist and with a student in a holy place.

Wendell Berry describes the grandmother of a character, Hannah Coulter, who speaks of the mentoring work accomplished mostly at Grandma's kitchen table, "She shaped my life, without of course knowing what my life would be. She taught me many things that I was going to need to know, without either of us knowing I would need to know them. She made the connections that made my life. . . . If it hadn't been for her, what would my life have been? I don't know. I know it surely would have been different."

Shaping Their Future is an invitation for you to acknowledge the role others have played in shaping your life, and it is a call to enter the arena yourself with others in the most formative moments of their lives. The university years provide what many look back on as setting a baseline for the formation of identity, vocation, and spirituality. It is not a technical skill but a hopeful willingness to engage and listen. It is a deep curiosity to see the face of the Artist in the unfolding story of the student seated beside you. It is reverence and awe for the living and breathing soul with whom you are privileged to walk. Let this book be a guide as you set forth on holy work for the sake of the Kingdom. It is rich with its own guidance for the sacred relationship you have with students.

Dr. Keith R. Anderson, President,
The Seattle School
of Theology and Psychology

Acknowledgments

This book has been "in process" for many years now and really has become an exploration of my own life development. I must thank many people, and I'm sure I will unknowingly leave someone out, but know that this book could never have seen the light of day without so, so many.

I would like to thank my family for all of their love and support throughout this process. To my sweet wife Heather, who has believed in me from the very beginning and been so understanding of my many late nights at the computer: thank you. You have helped me to become the husband I am today.

To my kids (Derek, Autumn, Kaiya, Noll, and Lailie) for being too young to really understand what's happening now but excited in their own ways for Daddy—simply because I'm excited. You're teaching me about what it means to be a dad.

To my parents, who have served as lifelong mentors, and especially my mom—for her willingness to review numerous early drafts of this book: thank you from the bottom of my heart.

I would also like to thank the many mentors who have helped to shape my own life and ministry throughout my journey. The list is too long to mention everyone, but Gary, Keith, Sherry, Alyson, Stu, and Ben deserve special thanks here.

I would like to thank the numerous students who have allowed me to come alongside them and walk for a season as a friend and mentor. You have taught me a lot about what it means to be both—in my successes and failures.

I would like to thank my peers and colleagues who continue to shape and sharpen me as a leader and mentor. I am especially thankful for those I have worked closely with: Lisa, Ashlee, Christy, and Micah. I'm equally grateful for the growing community at FaithONCampus.com and for those who have offered their insights and encouragements as they've read through early drafts of this book—most notably Tyler and Tiffany.

Finally, I would like to thank J. D., Andy, Holly, and all of the good folks at Seedbed Publishing. They have made this project possible through their willingness to take a chance on this first-time author. They have been a joy to work with and have been incredibly gracious and encouraging to me throughout the process.

God's richest blessings to you all as you continue to invest in His Kingdom through your roles as mentors—all in your own unique ways!

Grace and peace,
Guy

First Words

Nineteen years ago I was a college freshman, but I remember it as if it was yesterday. I was a relatively new Christ-follower and off to college without much of an idea about what was supposed to happen. I knew that I loved Jesus and wanted to make my faith central to my life, and part of my college experience, and so I started with an unusual openness to whatever God might have for me.

Now, for a few different reasons I use the word "unusual" to describe my openness to God at the outset of this new chapter in my life. First, as a new Christian, the idea of following Jesus was still a relatively unfamiliar idea to me. I made the decision to accept Jesus' gift of salvation while in high school, but, truthfully, I didn't know what it all meant. It had been made quite clear that this decision would impact my life after death, but there had been only faint allusions to how this decision should impact my life before death. So although I didn't really know what it meant or looked like, to follow Jesus in this lifetime, I believed there had to be something to it. So for this *sense* to be enough for me to be open to follow Jesus definitely qualified as unusual to me.

The second reason I suggest this was unusual was the fact that many of my peers, classmates who may have been followers of Jesus for most of their lives, didn't seem to live with the same kind of openness to Jesus. To look back, now, I can't tell you exactly what it was I saw or did not see in their lives. Or what I heard or did not hear in their words. But I could tell that many of them, as committed to Jesus as they might have claimed to have been, did not seem to be as open to following Jesus *wherever He might lead.* This wasn't (and isn't) a judgment on them. It was simply something that I noticed. And this *something* stood in stark contrast to *something else* I saw in the lives of a few guys I was getting to know.

> When I was a child, I talked like a child, I thought like a child, I reasoned like a child. When I became a man, I put the ways of childhood behind me.
>
> — Paul,
> 1 Corinthians 13:11

These guys are the third reason I classify this openness to God's leading as unusual: precisely because *they* were unusual. Now, I don't mean to suggest that they were the kind of weird or unusual that makes you want to pick up a stick, slowly back away, and then call the police from a safe distance. In fact, it was quite the opposite. What I saw in these guys was the kind of unusual that made you stop, take notice, and wonder what, *exactly,* was so unusual about them. I can now look back and recognize that the unusual I saw in these new friends—which made them unique, by comparison, to so many other college students on campus—was they had been living open to God for a number of years before we met. No, they weren't perfect, but they were authentic and persistent in their pursuit of Jesus. They were on the path that I wanted to be on, just a little farther down the way. And they were modeling for me, and others, a way to live life fully open to God.

I'm thankful to each of them for the ways they modeled faithful devotion to Jesus as college students. They were living proof that it was possible. Matt, Jon, Mike and Nate—you'll never fully know the ways that God used you in my life during those formative college years. I'm thankful for you and the parents, pastors, teachers and mentors who invested in you in the years leading up to (and through) the time we spent together on campus! I am forever changed because of it.

If you're wondering what this story has to do with this book, keep reading.

The Problem

The college years are some of the most formative in life. The context of the university campus is unlike any other—rich with educated voices, diversity, freedom, opportunity, and space to explore who you are and who you are becoming.

For far too many students today, however, the formative college years are being wasted. In a lot of ways college has become High School Part 2 but with a lot of debt incurred. While it was once assumed that youth will stay in school through the twelfth grade then go on to pursue further education *only* if it was required in order to obtain a specific job, this is no longer the case. For most of today's young people, the expectation is they will graduate from high school and go right into college, much like they transitioned from middle school to high school.

This being the case, a growing percentage of students are entering college without a clue of why they are there or what they are to do. Many have no clear sense of direction or purpose. Couple this with the retention of many of the same poor habits and attitudes they have toward coursework, as well as the low levels of responsibility that were present during their high school years, and you get too many of today's college students wasting some of the best years of their lives. As a result, they are not being shaped and formed in the ways that God desires for them. They are not making use of the formative environment and season of life that are the college years.

Moving toward Something Better

The college experience demands a transition, or series of transitions, and our young adults need to work with God to make the most of it. This book, designed for mentors of young people, is meant to serve the reader as a guide, a rudder, or even a springboard into specific arenas of life that require our students' attention, consideration, and application or action. It's about the rest of their lives and best utilizing some of the most formative years they'll ever have available to them. Now is the time for college students to co-labor with God to become the women and men they are intended to be!

>> *It takes a village to raise a child.*
> — African proverb

But it's not that easy, is it? The reality is, there's no one-size-fits-all (or even most) when it comes to making the most of the college years. No magical formula, or secret code, can make these years a grand success for each and every student.

Just as God has designed each one of us to be unique, I believe that the journeys we take—the journeys that students take—will also be unique. This means we're not looking for a map that comes with a start point, end point, and all of the best, predetermined "stops" along the way. Instead, we recognize that the specific start point is the place each student finds him or herself. We acknowledge that the end point is not the goal, but, instead, the journey itself is the goal, and therefore students need to be encouraged to live each day with great intention and purpose. Instead of offering students answers to their questions, we need to help them to ask the right kinds of questions. The kinds of questions that will open them up to the ways God wants to work in their lives. The kinds that will cause them to call into question the "outcomes" or "end destination" that the world around them has defined as "best."

As a professor, I often tell my Old Testament students that their questions may or may not be fully answered during the course of our semester together. I also let them know that their questions will likely lead them to more questions, bigger questions, and that although this might grow frustrating, it is a sign of God at work in our midst. I believe the same to be true about most of life. Jesus extends the same invitation to our students that He did His own: "Come, follow Me." He does not say where they will go, what they will do, how they will manage, or even what the "end result" might be. Instead, He creates space for questions, learning, formation, and even some struggle, pain, and chaos along the way. It's an invitation to an intentional journey that has the potential to change absolutely everything!

Why It Matters

Over the course of the next couple of chapters I'll attempt to outline why, exactly, it does matter that we *seize the day* and begin to reach out to today's college students in intentional ways.

The short of it is this:

> We are afforded some of the greatest opportunities
> here in America, and yet a growing percentage of
> our young people are not taking advantage of these
> opportunities. This is resulting in an increasing
> number of college graduates who are underprepared
> to care for themselves and contribute meaningfully
> to the world in which they live. Increasingly they
> lack the kind of faith that shapes them to their core,
> and this has ramifications in absolutely every area
> of their lives. Without direction, or the capacity
> to make good decisions, or even the ability to take

on meaningful levels of responsibility, these young adults will wander. They will struggle. And they will waste some of the best years of their lives.

I believe God is calling us—the parents, pastors, professors, coaches, directors et al. in the lives of these young people—to *step up* in some quite intentional ways! If we don't, who will? Our students are counting on us, whether they realize it or not.

This book may not provide the answers to all of the questions you have, but it will provide direction as you come alongside students and journey with them. I also want to invite you to check out http://faithoncampus.com, where I offer resources and meaningful conversations along these same lines, on a regular basis. Educating and equipping the next generation of young believers, and those who will come alongside them, is my life's calling.

Be encouraged, co-laborers in Christ, for you do not journey alone or work in vain. Don't hesitate to be in touch if I can assist you with anything. So let's come together, under the banner of Christ, and invest in our students as if our future depends on it! Because it does.

1
Emerging Adulthood

Students today are part of a generation falling behind developmentally—and academically, some would argue—and it has everything to do with *how* our students are approaching their formative years. For many students college has become High School Part 2. It's the *next thing*. For many it could just as easily (and accurately) be described as grades 13 through 16. Students continue on in their educational pursuits in a new context but retain many of the same ways of thinking and living they did in high school.

A new season of life has cropped up over the past thirty to forty years and has become known as Emerging Adulthood (or Prolonged Adolescence or Delayed Adulthood). It's a season that includes the college years on the front end and extends well into the late twenties for many of today's young people. I've actually seen, in some instances, where researchers have defined this season of life to extend to age thirty-two. Young people are no

---

The 5 Main Features of Emerging Adulthood

1. It is the age of identity explorations, of trying out various possibilities, especially in love and work.
2. It is the age of instability.
3. It is the most self-focused age of life.
4. It is the age of feeling in between, in transition, neither adolescent nor adult.
5. It is the age of possibilities, when hopes flourish, when people have an unparalleled opportunity to transform their lives.

— Dr. Jeffrey Arnett, *Emerging Adulthood*[1]

---

longer in the developmental stage of adolescence, but they've not yet come into their own in the realm of adulthood either. Some of this is because of their own choosing, and some of this has to do with the cultural environment that has been created for them. Regardless, it is a season of life that is reshaping the college experience in ways that are hindering the ultimate formation and development of today's young people.

High school graduates are heading off to college with many of the same attitudes, habits, and patterns they possessed in high school, without any sense that these things should change as a part of their new reality. As a result, the formative college years are becoming something much less than formative. To make matters worse, these young adults are incurring an overwhelming amount of debt in the process. So after four (or more) years as a college student, many are just as immature and undeveloped as they were when they first arrived on campus, with the only noticeable addition being the massive debt that takes on the form of a giant albatross hanging around their necks—severely weighing them down and further hindering their desire to "grow up," even after they graduate.

Much could be said about emerging adulthood, but for the sake of this book I'd like for us to think of it in terms of *freedom* and *responsibility*. Young people are enjoying many of the newfound freedoms that come with moving off to college (which has long been a part of the college experience) but are increasingly unwilling to acknowledge (or accept) the corresponding responsibilities that accompany those new freedoms (a defining characteristic of emerging adulthood). They want to fully enjoy all of the possibilities and decision-making power that come with being "out on their own," but they're uninterested (and in some instances, unable) to manage the "adult" responsibilities that come along with each freedom. And as you might imagine, it's causing tension and frustration in a variety of different contexts, while at the same time "stunting the growth" of these young people—during what are supposed to be some of the most formative years of their lives.

Add to this challenging scenario a few more elements: (1) a pop culture that fully supports the high freedom/low responsibility lifestyle, (2) a parenting paradigm that has sought to "be friends" with their kids and served to shelter them from struggle of any kind, and (3) the collective "hand-cuffing" of adults in relation to how they engage and challenge students. And the stage is set for a defunct college experience—at least in terms of students growing and maturing in many of the ways that they should.

American pop culture has long been about "self." Our culture sends a near-constant barrage of messages that tell us to "do what we want," "love what we do," and "indulge ourselves in whatever our hearts desire," which has served to create a generation (if not an entire culture) of self-obsessed individuals. We're losing (if not already lost) any sense of community or community obligation. We're losing our collective grasp on reality. So add a cultural endorsement of self-centeredness to a season of life (the college years) that is (by design) quite a self-centered experience, and we shouldn't be surprised to see what we see on campuses today. Sure, many students are able to see through the cultural façade of self (in some ways) and seize opportunities to serve others and be about the betterment of the collective campus community. But many of their peers struggle to see beyond the end of their noses, which only serves to further feed the ethos of emerging adulthood.

Many parents unknowingly serve as enablers to this season of Delayed Adulthood. We're currently seeing a generation of college students who were parented by individuals who had "distant" relationships with their own parents—their fathers in particular. Many of these individuals feel that their parents cheated them from having something more substantial in terms of a relationship. So they've made a conscious decision to offer their children (many of today's college students) a more personal, tangible parent/child relationship than the one they experienced. They decided to be friends with their children. They allowed their kids to overstep boundaries. They struggled to adequately challenge them to step into *responsibility*—a key word and concept to the overall argument I'm trying to make here. They failed to be a parent—something only they could be—and settled for being a friend, which most of their kids eventually grew to resent. Now, this isn't true for all of the parents of today's college students but a much larger percentage than ever before.

And yet, if you were to ask most parents if they want their college student to be *more* mature, *more* responsible, *more* capable, and *more* independent by the time they graduate from college, you'd undoubtedly get a near-unanimous "YES!" But far too many parents continue to (un)knowingly operate as the managers of their students' lives—even from a distance—during their formative college years. Instead of giving their student increasing levels of space—to make decisions on their own, pay for some of their own experiences, fight some of their own battles (take on more ownership and *responsibility* for their own lives)—they're doing these things for them. And it's not challenging today's students to handle some of these scenarios, or learn when they fail, and as a result it's stunting the developmental process. No, this isn't true for every student, but it is for far too many.

Equally troubling is an American culture that has made it difficult for nonparental types—like pastors, professors, coaches, and so on—to step in and really challenge students without fear of potential backlash from the parents. These probable mentor-types are being forced to operate with their hands tied behind their backs *until* a student grants them "permission" to speak into their lives. So would-be mentors hold back, bite their tongues, and don't interject themselves (in appropriate ways) into the lives of today's young people. Again, this isn't the reality in every instance but in far too many. I know this because I've seen it happening on campus, increasingly so, over the course of the past fifteen years.

Today's young people need to be challenged to step into adulthood now—and shown that it's a good thing, that it's the right "next step"—so that they can better utilize their formative college years. They need to understand that college is meant to be a one-time experience in which they truly transition into adulthood or, at the very least, get well on into the process. They need to understand that to waste these years is a great injustice and poor stewardship of an opportunity that much of the world does not have as readily available to them. The university experience needs to be seen, and therefore lived into, as the great gift that it is. Students need to be challenged to take responsibility for their lives, and the decisions they are making, knowing full well that more is at stake than just a diploma. It's about the rest of their lives!

THE MENTOR'S TOOLBOX

- What elements of emerging adulthood are you able to iden-tify in your students?
- Which of Arnett's five features is most challenging to you in terms of relating to this generation of young people?
- Where are you seeing students abuse "freedoms" and fail in the area of "responsibility"?
- Are you willing to be a mentor—*a part* of the solution?

Take some time to reflect on these questions in the space provided on the following page.

For further reading on the subject of emerging adulthood, consider:
- *Emerging Adulthood* by Jeffrey Arnett
- *Souls in Transition* by Christian Smith

Notes, questions, reminders,
points of action, etc.

2
Make a Difference

his chapter may feel out of place, at least at first.

Usually the "call to action" comes at the end of the book, after the problem was thoroughly discussed and a plan of action was clearly defined. And there will be such a call when we get to that point in this book. But it seemed appropriate, early on, that I invite you—the parent, pastor, professor, coach, director, or mentor-type—to take seriously the implications of allowing emerging adulthood to be a foregone conclusion in your students' lives.

Because I don't think it is.

I don't think it has to be.

I don't believe that *all* students will fall prey to five to fourteen years of wandering aimlessly about. I don't believe *all* students will struggle to find their way. I don't think *all* students will squander their formative college years. Yes, it's true, a growing percentage of them are, but I continue to see incredible students on campus, students who seem to be traveling the path (increasingly) less traveled. They are taking the more traditional journey toward adulthood that incorporates making good use of their college years, instead of treating them like throwaway years that don't really matter. Because the truth is, these years are incredibly important. No other season is quite like the college years—where students step out on their own for the first time in their lives and step into a context that is likely much more diverse than the one they come from, infused with well-educated faculty and staff who will expose them to new ideas and possibilities.

The college years are a convergence of a number of factors that make them catalytic! But they do require a bit of intentionality on the part of everyone involved.

An Invitation

For far too long now the voice of the Mentor (from here on out the word Mentor, whenever capitalized, will be inclusive of all mentor-types—i.e., parents, pastors, professors, coaches, directors, and the like) has been silent. We've sat idle and waited for students to give us permission to speak into their lives. We've waited, and watched, as students have struggled to make good choices, choose right priorities, care about the right things, and truly make good use of their formative college years. We've bitten our collective tongue and wondered when students will finally admit to themselves that they could benefit from a more "seasoned" voice in their lives then seek us out for what we have to offer.

And I fear that if we continue to wait on students to make the first move, we'll be waiting for a long time to come. And students will struggle as a result. No, not in all cases—as I said previously, there *are* students who are finding their way—but the percentage of students who fit into this category is shrinking with each year that goes by. Fewer and fewer students are coming to campus with a level of maturity and ability to prioritize (the right things) that set them up well for all of the potential that the college years engender. They need help navigating these incredibly formative years.

And that's where we come in.

We are positioned to assist them on this journey—to serve as a guide, a fellow traveler, a cheerleader when times get tough; a voice of reason when that's what is needed; and a personal soundboard for the countless things they are hearing, seeing, and experiencing.

> *We discover our identity in the context of community. We learn best together, with the help of other people.*
>
> — Keith R. Anderson and Randy D. Reese, *Spiritual Mentoring*[1]

Sure, some will struggle to *want* our seasoned insight, but most of them are simply waiting for *us* to invite them into this kind of relationship. Yep. That's right. They look at us and think, *They're so busy, why would they want to spend time with* me? While we're waiting on them, they're waiting on us—at least those who are aware enough of the role a Mentor can play in their lives. Some students will need to be convinced of this fact, and, yes, this is a part of our work as well.

We play our part, and students play their part.

Invite Students to Make a Difference in Their Own Lives

So the "call to action" on the front end of this book is to decide now whom you need to spend time with—and that you'll commit to do it—no matter how challenging or frustrating it might get along the way. Remember, it's a journey. And some students will need to be *convinced* that this journey is worth them giving their precious time and energy to. If they're not coming from a home or church that has helped them begin to recognize the importance of "growing up"—for a host of reasons that we will soon get to—then it's likely there will be some arm-twisting on the front end of this journey.

But the reality is, there are students—even if only a few—who are counting on *you* to invite them on this very journey. They don't know they need this, and may not need to know all of the details initially, but they will need to be extended an "invitation." They'll need to hear from you that you want to walk with them. That you care enough about them to spend some of your busy life simply sitting with them and getting to know them for the sake of seeing them succeed.

> » *Without a teachable heart, responsive and ready to learn, there will be little growth. Responsiveness is an active work of the mentoree, prior to meetings with the mentor as well as during the meetings.*
>
> — Anderson and Reese, *Spiritual Mentoring*[2]

The journeys and destinations will be different for all of the students we encounter so of course it would be silly for us to *prescribe* what success will look like. *Describing* what it could look like might be a better use of our energy.

"Success" is a relative term and will manifest itself in different ways from one student to the next. But at its core, "success" in this case is centered on students beginning to take seriously their own lives. It will include the beginning of a transition that involves students taking on more ownership and responsibility for their lives through the decisions they make about things that really matter. It will entail establishing important priorities that will be life giving and formative during their fertile college years.

And here's the kicker: it will *require* that *students choose* to begin the journey and do the work only *they* can do. We do our work, but only they can do theirs—and this strikes against emerging adulthood at its core. Also, this is the place where students will choose to take the path less traveled, or to follow the steady stream of students down the path of prolonged adolescence, skirting responsibility however possible and neglecting to transition in the ways that college is designed to help facilitate.

We do our work; students must do their work, and we must allow God to do the work that *only* He can do.

The Third Part of the Equation

We've acknowledged that, as Mentors, we have to become better initiators with students. We need to become more aware of our role in the lives of today's college students and step into that role. We've also established the fact that students have a significant role in their growth and development during their formative college years. They *need* to play an active and ever-present role in their own maturation and formation. But there's another part of this equation. In fact, it's the most significant part of this dynamic equation.

God.

Without God, all of the efforts that we make as Mentors, and the efforts of our students, will amount to something human sized. It will be *something*, but it will be lacking, for sure. When we invite God into this process, however, things change. In fact, everything changes because we realize that we are but a small part in the process. We have a role, and our students have a role, but it's God who has the ultimate role in this process.

God makes growth and development truly transformational! He's bigger than any of us. He impacts us at the core of who we are—and changes us from the inside out. I think the apostle Paul captured this idea as he addressed the Christians in Corinth:

> What, after all, is Apollos? And what is Paul? Only
> servants, through whom you came to believe—as
> the Lord has assigned to each his task. *I planted the*

seed, Apollos watered it, but God has been making it grow. So neither the one who plants nor the one who waters is anything, but only God, who makes things grow. *The one who plants and the one who waters have one purpose,* and they will each be rewarded according to their own labor. For we are God's co-workers; you are God's field, God's building. (1 Corinthians 3:5–9, emphasis added)

Paul wrote on an issue of allegiance with these early Christians, who seemed to be fighting over whom to follow—who deserved their loyalty? Paul was quick to set the record straight. It wasn't Paul, and it wasn't Apollos but God. Both Paul and Apollos played a role in the Corinthians' lives, they both had a job to do, but it was the Triune God who ultimately took their mustard seed of faith and began to grow it into a developing faith. Because of this, it was Jesus (and not Paul or Apollos) who was worthy of their allegiance and loyalty.

And the same is true here.

We have a role in this process, and so do students. But it's the ever-present work of the Spirit of God that we must be willing to yield to in this process. Mentors and students come together, both with a desire to give to the process and each in their own ways, but it's God who will ultimately work in the ways (and timing) that He desires. We cannot manipulate God to work, nor can we manufacture godlike growth in our students. But, if we're collectively faithful in giving ourselves to this process, there's no telling how God might choose to work and move in our midst.

Ten Key Areas of Responsibility

What follows in the rest of this book is a look at what I believe to be ten of the most important conversations (and areas of growth and transition) that students need to engage during their formative college years. Starting with faith and constructing a worldview; to how they understand college, money, responsibility, and their past; and then on to how they might better live in their peer relationships, pursuit of intimacy, relationships with people who are "different" from them, as well as how they might relate to those mentor-types who want to come alongside them.

If we can introduce students to these themes and help them to start to intentionally engage these areas, then their college years will become the kind of transformational experience that we believe is possible. Sure, there might be other areas that students could benefit from focusing on, but over the course of the past fifteen years I've spent on four different college campuses (spanning three different denominations), these are the areas that seem to be *most* in need of our students' attention.

And here's why.

Congruence in Thought, Belief, and Action

In the end, we will *not* have a finished product. Yes, by the time our students graduate, they will still be a work in progress but, with hope, one much further along in the process of "growing up" because of the time they (we) intentionally spent in pointed conversations exploring the themes mentioned above (and in the chapters that follow). And over the course of our years of conversing, there will be a progression taking shape (God willing). A new way of *seeing, understanding*, and *living* within the world. This change will have to do with how we help students to better connect their thinking with their beliefs, and ultimately the way(s) they then choose to live in the world.

Too many of today's students are failing to connect the dots between these three things: thought, belief, and action. The things we think about shape what we believe, and what we believe shapes how we live. And I think we'd be remiss to not acknowledge the ever-present Enemy who plots against our students making these kinds of connections, and developments ("The thief comes only to steal and kill and destroy," John 10:10a).

In some cases students are thinking about harmful (or unhelpful) things that are warping the way(s) they believe, which ultimately has a damaging effect on how they live. In other cases, students think about the right things, and for some it may even translate into a right way of believing, but ultimately there seems to be a disconnect, a lack of congruence for most of today's students between thought, belief and action.

>> *This becomes the primary task of the mentor: to awaken the mentoree to his or her uniqueness as a loved child of God, created in the image of God for intimacy of relationships that empowers the individual for authentic acts of ministry.*

— Anderson and Reese, *Spiritual Mentoring*[3]

Too many students are able to hold (in tension) conflicting realities. They believe the truth about Jesus but fail to live as if it really matters. They think that drinking and drugs are no good—and only lead to bad places—yet choose to make them a central tenet of their weekend plans. They want to save themselves sexually for their someday spouse but choose to engage in the hookup culture, believing that it's the only way they can experience love and intimacy *now*.

This breakdown in thinking, believing, and living speaks to the lack of ownership and responsibility that a growing percentage of students are willing to take for their lives. It speaks to a generation who the Enemy is deceiving. And although the thief has come to "steal and kill and destroy," we must remember—and make known—that Jesus came "that they my have life, and have it to the full" (John 10:10b).

So let's get to it! A generation of college students is desperate to know that there is a better way of living, and this will require our intentional time and thoughtful investment in their lives.

THE MENTOR'S TOOLBOX

- What most excites you about taking a more intentional mentoring role in the lives of your student(s)? What reservations do you have?
- What hurdles do you anticipate in getting your student(s) to buy in to this kind of process? What reservations might you anticipate them having? How might you be able to proactively speak to some of those potential reservations?
- What most excites you about recognizing God's part in this developmental process? What most challenges you?

Take some time to reflect on these questions in the space provided on the following page.

For further reading on the subject of mentoring, consider:
- *Spiritual Mentoring* by Keith Anderson and Randy Reese
- *One.Life* by Scot McKnight

Notes, questions, reminders,
points of action, etc.

Faith

Irrelevant » Peripheral » Central

There is a way that appears to be right,
but in the end it leads to death.
— Proverbs 14:12

Trust in the LORD with all your heart
and lean not on your own understanding;
in all your ways submit to him,
and he will make your paths straight.
— Proverbs 3:5-6

O f all the content that will be explored in this book, this is the material that we need "to get," and help students to get! Faith: it's the beginning, middle, and end of everything that really matters. If students miss this, if they fail to engage this as central to their college experience, then the rest of what is explored will not be understood in the correct context. For it is God, and God alone, who is able to shape them and form them over the course of their journeys. We are simply agents of information and conversation—possible guides along the journey, for a season. Faith, as significant as it is to their lives in its entirety, is especially significant for their formative college years. And faith is a big enough conversation (and so central to the focus of this work—and the development of today's college students) that it requires two different chapters (if not more).

Before we can have serious conversations with students about growing in their faith, it seems an increasing percentage of college students actually need to be convinced that this conversation (not to mention faith itself) is actually worth having.

Statistically speaking, America is becoming less and less "religious." Many would say that we now live in a *post-Christian* America. More and more families are opting out of church and other faith-forming activities, which means that young people are not being exposed (at least not with any consistency) to the story of God and Jesus, to biblical and theological teaching, and to the exploration of truth and meaning within a religious context. We, as a country, are putting our faith, hope, and trust in other things. This is shaping how today's young people develop, make decisions, understand their purpose in life, and view the future.

Add to this the fact that, for quite some time now, college has been a place where many young people have gone and "lost their faith," and you can see how the centrality of faith during the formative college years is becoming an increasingly challenging task. A part of the reason for this is that those who arrive on campus with some level of faith have left the support systems and structures of faith (i.e., their family and/or home church) and failed to find something to replace them with.

For others, this "departure from faith" actually exposes a deficiency in the young students' discipleship leading up to their college years, which speaks to a major shortcoming in churches in the past decade. Students are dry and have a frail faith that doesn't amount to much more than a cobbled-together list of beliefs or Bible passages patch-worked together by well-intentioned parents, grandparents, pastors, youth pastors, and spiritual mentors from their past. When students make their way to campus, this "thin" faith quickly crumbles under the weight of opposition, or exposure to beliefs that are different from the ones they hold.

In survey after survey, the majority of Americans describe themselves as Christians. . . . But that connection is often shallow and on the surface, having more to do with cultural identification than it does with deep faith.

— David Kinnaman, *You Lost Me*[1]

Other students enter the culture of campus life and struggle to see how faith fits into the equation. It made sense back home, and many students are able to see how it "fit in" to *that* scheme of life. But in this new context, that same faith is failing to translate. New relationships, experiences, and ideas begin to expose some of the "holes" in what had once seemed like quite a thoughtful set of beliefs. Or, it's quite possible that it's not holes that are exposed as much as it is a growing tension between what the student believes and how they want to live in this new environment. Either way, maintaining faith becomes a huge challenge.

Still others simply come to realize that they never really "had" a faith of their own; they were simply riding the coattails of their parents or grandparents or friends who were talking with them and trying to get them to church every week. They may have attended worship services with some consistency, but it really had more to do with following "house rules," making someone else happy, or it even represented an honest pursuit of truth, purpose, and hope. In their new context, however, other priorities take over and a *shadow* faith is boxed up and put in the back of the closet.

In order to help students make the very most of their college experience, we need to, as quickly as possible, help them to understand the relevance—the significance—of having faith during these very formative years of life. As we engage them, and begin to sense an openness and/or receptivity to this conversation, we need to challenge students to begin to explore (i.e., ask questions, seek answers, and "try it out" in their everyday lives), such that it begins to shape who they are and how they live. If we're able to make inroads here, the next step is to challenge them to give all of themselves to God—or put another way, to allow God to become the very center of their lives such that He impacts the decisions they make and the direction their lives take in absolutely every arena of their lives.

Irrelevant

My own faith journey started in the realm of irrelevance and remained so during most of my growing-up years. I was born to two loving parents who had themselves grown up in nominally Christian homes. As a child, my mother attended a Methodist church—and that was about the extent of it. My father grew up attending a Catholic church and even a private, Catholic school for his elementary school education, and that was about the extent of it for him. Neither one of them really saw faith "lived out" in their homes.

So it made sense when it came to raising my brothers and me that (1) my parents decided we should be raised consistently attending church, (2) they would raise us in a Lutheran church (because apparently that's a good middle ground when you cross a Methodist with a Catholic), and (3) it was never anything *we* saw lived out in *our* home during our growing up years.

In all of my childhood years of regularly attending church, I cannot recall ever understanding why I was really there, or why it even mattered. I sang the songs, colored the pictures, and listened to stories and lessons. I even went through three and a half years of confirmation classes (and was ultimately "confirmed"). But no one ever sat me down and talked to me about God's grand story, the saving work of Jesus, the Spirit-filled life—or why any of it mattered.

So for me, during my growing-up years, church was quite simply the reason I couldn't sleep in on Sunday morning. It was the event that preceded a late Sunday breakfast with extended family, and Confirmation class was a painfully boring three-hour class that consumed far too many Wednesday evenings during my middle-school years.

Faith made no sense, so obviously its relevance was lost on me. It's not that I was "too smart" for faith and simply wouldn't allow myself to believe something that required me to have "faith," but more so that nobody ever helped me to connect the dots—and I apparently didn't care enough to force the issue.

> > >

Every student's upbringing is different. Introductions to church and faith, whether they happen or not, do different things for different youth. Some find meaning while others won't. Some start an earnest faith journey, while others don't even know such an opportunity exists. Some find the church to be a welcoming and safe place, while many others find it to be a place of judgment, rule-keeping, and facades. Yet by the time most students are heading toward our campuses, they have identified a god in their lives. It may be the Living God, but for many that's not the case. Instead, their god—what influences many of their decisions and direction in life—is something far less worthy of the position and weight that it holds. The pursuit of money, power, pleasure, fame, influence, possessions, or something equally insufficient and subservient is given a position of authority in their lives, ultimate authority.

>> *19.6% of Americans claim no religious affiliation (up nearly 5% in the past 5 years).*

33% of Americans under the age of 30 claim no religious affiliation. And 88% of this population claims no desire to find a religion that suits their needs.

— www.pewforum.org[2]

And so students go about their college experience with this god serving as the final checkpoint in *what, how,* and *why* they prioritize. It becomes the lens through which everything else is filtered. It shapes the way they see themselves, other people, and ultimately the world. And it's *not* good, which is why we need to help students recognize the difference between their little, insufficient, and false god and the true, all-loving, and all-powerful Triune God—and *why* it matters.

But how?

Well, some of that depends on the role that you play in their lives. Some of you, given your unique role, will have the opportunity to engage students through a number of different ministry initiatives. Your role is to extend the invitation—in fact, countless invitations—and to help students believe that you and your ministry are a safe place to ask questions, explore doubts, pursue truth, and be "known" and accepted just as they are while on the journey.

Many more of you will have to look for the windows of opportunity that are given. It may come in the hallway, between classes, or it may come after practice or rehearsal; still, others will have to prayerfully wait for that inquisitive (or distressed) phone call that starts down a winding path of question upon question. And others of you may feel called to take more initiative in creating space and opportunity for conversations about life and faith. But regardless of *when* or *where* or *how* or *why*, students will need to be encouraged to grapple with the relevance of faith—especially during their formative college years—and we need to be prepared to share our own story of finding faith—and the differences it's made in our own lives.

Nothing is more powerful than personal testimony. And it doesn't have to be the dramatic "I was into drugs," "I got someone pregnant," or even the "I spent some time in jail" kind of testimony, the "overcoming all the odds" testimony that we tend to believe holds all the power. The reality is, most of our students aren't coming from a wild background themselves. But in the comfort and security of the U.S., the "need" for faith can easily be lost on most.

So our first task, as Mentors looking to see this generation of college students make the most of their formative college years, is to help them recognize their need for faith—especially during college (because we know that if they have it, and grow it, during their formative college years, then it will not only shape them in these years but likely for much of their life that follows). We can't force anything. And yet, we cannot skip over this crucial element in order to get to the other important content in this book. Faith must be the starting point and the foundation from which everything else is understood. We'll talk more about a "life lens," or worldview, in chapter 4, but for now we need to realize that everything hinges upon helping students to begin to engage the idea that faith is relevant.

Peripheral

I've never understood the purpose of having a faith that's compartmentalized off on the edge of one's life somewhere, only to be visited every now and again, when it's time to make a deposit or withdrawal. And as a relatively new Christian, I was especially surprised to find that in my peers when I attended college—a *Christian* college, of all places. I couldn't comprehend why people would choose to attend a school so geared toward helping them to grow and mature in their faith if they weren't really all that interested in engaging most (or even some) of the opportunities that were being afforded us.

Yes, I was a new believer and felt the need (hopefully it was more desire than need) to take advantage of almost every opportunity made available to me at the Christian college I attended. Worship services, small groups, mission trips, and so forth. It was all I could do to fit in other things, such as classes. It was a spiritual boot camp of sorts, and I loved it! Strangely, however, I felt like I was in the minority in that regard. The longer I was on campus, the more it seemed that the students I encountered were "serious" about their faith—and could talk circles around me, theologically speaking—but when it came to prioritizing their time, faith-forming opportunities seemed to be low on the list of things to do.

It didn't make sense to me.

But in the fifteen years since I graduated from college— having worked on campuses all but six months of that time—I've come to better understand what I was experiencing as a wide-eyed coed who functioned like a spiritual sponge, absorbing everything that came within reach. I was hungry. I was eager. It was new to me. I was in the "honeymoon" stage of my faith, and most of my peers were not. My faith was the center of my world, but it had ceased to be so for many of the students I shared campus with, or so it seemed.

> > >

A lot of "Christians" live with a *compartmentalized* faith. They've made some decisions about what they believe about Jesus, likely verbalized a profession of faith at some point in time, but now live life with a faith that doesn't seem to make much of a day-to-day difference. They believe because they think it's supposed to make a difference in their lives—or maybe, more accurately, their death. Craig Groschell refers to these Christians as "Christian Atheists," stating "they believe in Jesus, but then live as if He doesn't exist." This sounds harsh, but the reality is sobering. Many of us who claim to be followers of Jesus tend to compartmentalize our faith such that we only access it when we're at church, or with certain groups of people, but truthfully don't really allow it to function at our core being. It's *peripheral*. It means something but not everything.

So it shouldn't surprise us that many of the students showing up on campus today operate in this same way. This is what many of them have grown up seeing in their churches or homes. It means something but not everything. It's relevant—but only to a certain extent. When I talk with students on campus about this, I typically use a simple illustration to make this point. I start by drawing two circles. I divide the first circle like a pizza pie. I draw the second circle to look like a wagon wheel. I then place the word "faith" in one of the segments in the first circle and place it in the center circle of the second circle. Like this:

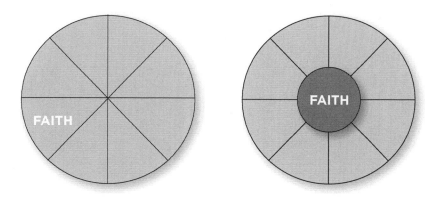

From here, I try to help students to see the difference between living a compartmentalized life (represented by the circle on the left, where faith touches the edge of a couple areas of our lives) and living one where our faith in Jesus is at the center (as represented by the circle on the right, where it's at the core and touches every other area of life). When we live a compartmentalized life, we relegate our faith to a particular segment of our life, and therefore limit the influence it has on all of the other "segments" of our life. If we were to fill in all of the other segments of the pizza pie, the only other segments that our faith would have influence on are the segments on either side of the faith segment.

When you contrast that with the circle on the right, where faith is not only central but touches (influences) every other segment of the circle (representing our life), you can begin to understand the distinction, and better see how drastically different *that* kind of life would be.

This is a challenge that all Christians face—to keep their faith from becoming compartmentalized and allow it to (from the very center of their being) shape every part of them. Students need help with this all the more. Compartments are neat. Compartments are easier to define, and understand. Compartments give *students* control, or at least the illusion of control. But when students put God in a box, they limit God's ability to work in their lives. And while this may seem the "safer" of the two choices, especially during the college years, the reality is that the formative nature of these years necessitate that students allow God full reign.

This kind of life requires sacrifice—the kind of sacrifice that many college students are unwilling to make because it *limits* their own freedom, which is something they're just now really getting a taste for. But if, and when, they're able to make this shift from a faith that's peripheral to one that's central, then we'll see them begin to blossom in ways for which only God could be credited.

Central

Can you remember the first time you encountered one of those Christians who *truly* lived as if they believed Jesus was real, and meant what He said as revealed in the Bible? And it wasn't a way of living that was based on a fear of what "The Almighty" might do if they stepped out of line but, instead, a way of living that seemed free, life giving, and joy filled.

Have you ever met a Christian like that?

I did. Before I even knew how to comprehend what I was experiencing.

He's now one of my dearest friends. Back then, however, he was an unknown in my eighth grade music class. As a middle-schooler, he stood out amidst a sea of awkward, insecure, and inconsistent classmates as someone who was comfortable in his own skin (an incredible feat in middle school), peaceful and fun. I can't say that I had ever encountered anyone like him before. I didn't know him, but I knew that I wanted to.

Matt and I started to hangout a little at school, and the summer before we entered high school we started to hangout a bit more. He continued to puzzle me, and so did his family because they were just as "weird" as he was. But it didn't end there. That summer Matt also introduced me to some of his friends. One in particular, Jon, may have been even weirder than my new friend Matt, and so was *his* family.

They were happy, loving people, but it was more than that. It eluded me for much of the first two years of our new friendship; that is, until I accepted the gift of grace and salvation that Jesus extends us all while at a summer camp—with Matt and Jon.

Then things started to come into focus.

It wasn't that they were weird as much as it was that they were loving followers of Jesus, and He was shining brightly through each of them. They had each decided to let Jesus invade their lives to its very core, and change them from the inside out. It was nothing that could be manufactured or faked. Each was a life transformed or, more accurately put, transform*ing*.

Their priorities were different, as was their outlook on life. Their joy didn't ebb and flow with the changing tide of their circumstances; it was pure and consistent. No, they weren't perfect, but they didn't need to be. They had something that I wanted, and eventually found in Jesus.

> > >

A life *transforming*.

How great does that sound?

And the truth is, *all* students are a work in progress—a life transforming. Yet not all students will experience the same kind of growth and formation during their college years. Why? Because some will choose to invest in this process, while others will not. Some students will choose to make their faith central to their college experience, which will unlock the doors to an entirely different way of being shaped and formed, while others will not. And this is *HUGE*.

We want students to get to the place where they are making their faith so central to life that they are in a consistent process of being transformed, from the inside out. But for many students it's an extensive and challenging journey to get to this place, one that not many are ready and willing to make. They will need to be willing to sacrifice a lot. They will need to take on and embrace a different set of priorities. Living a *Christ*-centered life in a "*me*"-centered culture is quite a challenging thing to do. And yet, college students seem to have some of the greatest potential to make this jump specifically because they are in such a grand season of transition and formation. In many ways, everything in their lives is "on the table." And that's why our work with them— our willingness to make them a priority, and come alongside them in some intentional ways—is so important.

Today's culture does not naturally move them toward this kind of Christ-centered life. In fact, it does just the opposite. And that's why I decided to write this chapter (3.1), before the next chapter on faith (3.2). After I had written chapter 3.2, I realized that we needed to have this first conversation (or series of conversations) with students before we can have the next. Our task is to help students see the importance, the significance, of a life of faith. And a life of faith doesn't see faith as an "add-on" but as central to one's identity. A compartmentalized faith—that is only accessed at certain times, with certain people, for certain reasons—is a faith that is unable to have the kind of transformational impact that God desires. It becomes an activity, an option, an adjective among many others that can be chosen from.

> *Spiritual formation is a process of being conformed to the image of Christ for the sake of others.*
> — M. Robert Mulholland
> *Invitation to a Journey*[3]

Faith, for Christians, needs to be central to who we are and how we live. We and others must model this for our students before they can envision what we're talking about here. And if you're honest, that's probably what scares you most about being a Mentor—feeling as if you're not "good enough" or that you should have it "more together" or even that there have got to be "more qualified" Mentors for your student(s) to spend time with. And while having a healthy and honest assessment of ourselves is important, believing that we are unworthy of serving as a Mentor to a young person is a lie we need not believe.

We are all on our own journey with God. And what matters most as we look to serve as a guide and faithful companion to students (who are also on a journey) is that we: (1) tend faithfully to our own relationship with God, and (2) that we remember that we are not perfect (and never will be this side of heaven) but are a work in progress, like our students.

THE MENTOR'S TOOLBOX

- Can you recall your own journey from seeing faith as irrelevant to peripheral to central? What do you remember most about those different stages?
- Do you remember what it took to transition from one of those stages to the next? Was it an experience? Something you saw lived out in another believer? A timely conversation that helped things to "click" in your own mind?
- What is the biggest challenge you currently face in living out a faith that is central, and not peripheral, to your life?

Take some time to reflect on these questions in the space provided on the following page.

Here are several questions that might help to promote conversation with your student in this area:

- Is faith important to you? Why or why not?
- What kind of role does faith play in your life? Why is it that way? What influences or experiences in your life have caused you to understand and/or experience faith in this way?
- Have you ever thought about how your faith could play a bigger role in your life? Does this idea scare you? Excite you? Why?
- How does your faith inform how you live? Do your beliefs about God, Jesus, and the Holy Spirit shape the decisions you make? If so, how?
- Do you have any spiritual heroes or role models? If so, what is it about them that most impresses you? Are there ways in which you see them live faith out that you hope to emulate in your own life?

For further reading on the subject of faith among Emerging Adults, consider:

- *You Lost Me* by David Kinnaman
- *UnChristian* by Gabe Lyons and David Kinnaman
- *College Ministry in a Post-Christian Culture* by Stephen Lutz

Notes, questions, reminders,
points of action, etc.

Faith

Family Faith » Owned Faith » Growing Faith

Consider it pure joy, my brothers and sisters,
whenever you face trials of many kinds, because you know
that the testing of your faith produces perseverance.
Let perseverance finish its work so that you may be mature
and complete, not lacking anything.

— James 1:2-4

Now faith is confidence in what we hope for
and assurance about what we do not see.
This is what the ancients were commended for.
By faith we understand that the universe was formed
at God's command, so that what is seen
was not made out of what was visible.

— Hebrews 11:1-3 NIV

During the first eighteen years of life young people are heavily influenced by their parents, grandparents, aunts and uncles, pastors, teachers, mentors, and coaches in a number of life-shaping ways—not the least of which is their faith. Every upbringing being different, this faith is likely taught, talked about, and modeled in a variety of ways, to varying levels and degrees, and for a host of different reasons. Young people are often taught what to believe (most of the time), why to believe it (some of the time), and even how to live it out (almost none of the time)—and at some point during their growing-up years they are expected to accept this faith, claim it as their own, and attempt to faithfully live it out. And while some will, others won't, and this will be where their faith journey ends, or so it would seem.

The college years often serve as a natural time of transition for young people of faith. Statistics say that the transition is not a positive one. In fact, a recent article by the Barna Group reported that "a majority of twentysomethings—61% of today's young adults—had been churched at one point during their teen years but they are now spiritually disengaged (i.e., not actively attending church, reading the Bible, or praying). Only one-fifth of twentysomethings (20%) have maintained a level of spiritual activity consistent with their high school experiences."[1] The need to come alongside students during this formative season in some intentional, disciple-making ways couldn't be more real!

In the previous chapter I established the need for faith during the college years. In this chapter I'd like to focus our thinking in the area of faith development. Those college students choosing not to totally abandon their faith, shelving it for the foreseeable future (i.e., the college years and beyond), at first might be slow to wander too far from their *family faith* (or the faith they've inherited from their family). However, they will eventually feel the need to spread their wings and move toward something that is a bit more personal, more *owned*—or need to be encouraged to do so. Taking on "ownership" of one's faith involves a level of intentionality in terms of:

- Asking hard questions (even scary questions),
- Searching diligently for answers (without trying to steer the outcomes),
- Learning how to be OK with (some) unanswered questions (this is one of the places that faith will grow its roots down deep), and
- Ultimately coming to some conclusions of their own.

All of this may, or may not, land them close to the family faith that they arrived on campus with.

For some students, this journey will prove to be too great or, sadly, unworthy of their attention, and they'll never make it beyond their family faith, never really claim their faith for themselves. Other students will do the hard work of seeking, and even finding, but then choose to stop at this point of having an *owned faith*, content to live life with their new set of beliefs—a faith they can claim full ownership of—but in so doing they will have quit "the journey" after only just having started. Upon claiming ownership of their faith, it will be time to recognize that living in relationship with Jesus is not as simplistic as deciding on what to believe. It involves investing in this relationship with Jesus, which will include highs and lows, triumphs and failures, growth and formation, pain and struggle, mystery and uncertainty, life and joy. And it must go on for a lifetime. Yes, a *growing faith* will require much, but it will provide *so* much more! But let's start back at the beginning.

Family Faith

My own faith journey started in earnest during the summer between my sophomore and junior years of high school when I accepted Jesus as Lord of my life. I asked Him to forgive me of my sins, begin a process of changing my heart and life, and to use me—somehow—whatever that might mean or look like. I was at a weeklong summer camp, the first I had ever attended; and while I couldn't really comprehend the full magnitude of what I was experiencing, I *did* know my life would be different from that moment forward. Although I had grown up in the church, attending Sunday school and later Confirmation classes, *my* reality was that it had never really meant anything to me.

The truth is, I grew up in a home where going to church was just something we did, for no apparent reason. It was something our family did before joining our extended relatives for a late breakfast. It was the reason I couldn't sleep in on Sunday mornings. It was a place to sing and be told about God and Jesus, but no one ever helped me to comprehend, or even care about, what I was hearing. And while there may have been more the church could have done to "reach me," much of how I understood faith— or *didn't* understand faith—had to do with my parents and how they understood, and ultimately lived out, their faith.

It wasn't until sometime during my college years, as I was beginning to grow and mature in my faith, that I asked my parents more about their own faith (or what I perceived to be a total lack thereof). I found out that my mom grew up attending a Methodist church, while my dad attended a Catholic church and grade school. But their attendance, much like my own, never amounted to much of anything. This sort of "Sunday faith" seemed to be what was modeled to them throughout their growing-up years, so it made complete sense that this was how they modeled faith to my brothers and me.

And although my childhood church experience wasn't doing much for me, I can look back and recognize God beginning to work in my life sometime during my eighth-grade year—in choir class, of all places. As a result of some shifting friendships, and a chance encounter in that choir class, I was exposed to something *different* that served to open me to seeing faith from a totally different perspective.

In the First Words section of this book I mentioned some "unusual" friends. This is a story of the first one I met. His name was Matt. Somehow our paths had never crossed during our seventh-grade year, at least not that I can recall. Matt sat a few chairs down from me, and there was just something *off* about him, something different. I couldn't figure out what it was (and quite honestly, as an eighth-grade boy, I'm not so sure that I cared enough to put a lot of detective work into it), but I was intrigued and knew I wanted to get to know him beyond our shared disdain for choir class. By the end of the school year we had indeed become friends—and little did I know that God was at work, preparing the soil of my life for seeds to be planted.

The summer that followed I began to hang out with Matt and some of his friends, over at his house. The strangeness with which I had once perceived Matt (but clearly had gotten over) was now coming at me in consistent waves—through Matt's family and friends. I still couldn't put my finger on it, but these people were different—nice, but it was a different kind of nice, and I didn't know whether I wanted to make a run for it—or never leave. Probably it wasn't until sometime after my conversion experience, a couple of summers later, that I realized just what I was experiencing in these people: the love of Christ. It was warm. It was caring. It was accepting, no matter what. It was infectious. And it was *different* from what I had experienced at home or church.

Now let me be quick to say that I grew up in quite a loving home. I have two of the greatest parents a person could ever be lucky enough to be born to, and raised by. But as loving as they were, and as loving a home as they created for our family, it was still different from what I experienced in my friend Matt's home.

> > >

Our families of origin, or the families in which we are born and raised, shape us in ways we will feel for the rest of our lives. For better and for worse we cannot choose our initial families. Nor can we choose the ways in which our parents will raise us. Likewise, we cannot choose the ways in which they will shape our understanding of who God is, what Jesus did and died for, and why it should matter to us. So much of *what* they chose to instill in us, as well as the reasons behind *why* they chose it, is tied to the ways in which they were raised. In many instances, parents are simply repeating what their own parents did for them, and doing it in the same way(s).

In other instances, parents make intentional decisions to raise their own children in ways that are *quite* different from what they themselves experienced during their growing-up years. This was true of my parents, in a number of areas, but not this area of faith. Regardless of *how* it occurs, or *why*, the reality is that it does indeed occur. Over the course of the first eighteen years of life, young people are shaped, formed, taught, and trained by their parents, teachers, mentors and pastors—what to think, what to believe, and how to live. Then most of them leave this familiar environment and head to the university campus, where this family faith is going to be put to the test. This is where new Mentor-types will need to step in, and old Mentor-types will likely need to reconsider their approach to investing in the lives of their college students.

As I stated above, both positives and negatives result from eighteen years of being conditioned on *what* and *why* and *how* to believe. On the upside, our families (and trusted others) provide us with a foundation of belief that serves as a starting point, even should we decide one day that we're going to scrap the whole thing and start over. Our early exposure to faith—of any kind— also helps to provide us with a level of comfort, or familiarity, with the things of God. Whether it's as simple as names and stories from the Bible or how to read the Bible and pray, or even something a little more involved like serving the poor and understanding justice, exposure at any level will provide a point of reference and familiarity for moving forward. Finally, I suggest that through any exposure to religion, or religious living, we are also given a variety of models for how things can (or should) be lived out. From our parents to our pastors, our mentors to extended relatives, everyone will likely have something slightly (or even dras-tically) different to share regarding: what kind of church to attend, how

Our families of origin, or the families in which we are born and raised, shape us in ways we will feel for the rest of our lives. **«**

often to read the Bible, how to pray, when and why to pray, and so on. Regardless of what we thought of it during our growing-up years, we can take positives from our family faith. One of the roles of Mentors during this season of life is to help students explore their family faith and acknowledge (if not celebrate) those things that have been meaningful and formative in their growing-up years.

Likewise, some negatives serve to hinder our faith develop-ment during the college years because of some of the ways we were exposed to faith during our growing-up years. For some of us our immersion into religion at a young age left us feeling as if we had all of the answers, and there's really not much more to explore in this area. We've learned it all, at least well enough, and now it's time to explore new things (i.e., move on from this topic). For others it may be about a bad experience—in church or a strictly religious household—and as a result there is a strong desire to make a clean break from the family faith, as soon as possible. Still others find that the overly casual nature of their family faith during their growing-up years left them struggling to understand how faith fits into this new season of life, if at all. Mentor-types, during the formative college years, have the obligation of helping students to make this jump—or at least help them to see that they don't have to throw the proverbial baby out with the bathwater. It's not our role to convince them of anything but, instead, to help them to remain "open" to God during this important time of life.

What does this family faith look like once it arrives on campus? Well, I'm sure that it will vary somewhat from student to student, but ultimately it will look like the thoughts, ideas, and beliefs of other people were placed in one of the college-bound bags and shipped off to campus with the rest of their stuff—with the thought that it will be welcomed and tended to in this new place. Many students won't necessarily know why they need this prepackaged set of beliefs, or what good they might do them in this new place, but for some reason most will not be quick to discard them. And so here they are, on campus, with all of the uncertainty that surrounds this boxed faith. Many students will find a safe place, somewhere out of the way, to store this set of beliefs until the day arrives when they sense the need to call upon them for some reason. Many have been led to believe that these beliefs are important, that they mean something, and so they hold them as treasure but quietly struggle to understand how they could hold any true value.

Locked away, these beliefs typically stay until some dramatic, drastic, or even tragic event occurs. When it does, many students will go running to that mental treasure chest where they've safely stowed their inherited beliefs—perhaps to find pure gold. They'll dust them off, hoping beyond hope that those beliefs will provide the necessary answers for what they're currently facing. Sadly, in those moments of frail humanity, students often find that the beliefs they sit with seem hollow and unfamiliar, even unrecognizable. It's not that they're bad beliefs, or wrong beliefs, but they're not *their* beliefs. They're someone else's. And now students are left struggling to know how to access God in that moment, and what to make of those beliefs they had been given, which leads them to second-guessing whether there's even a god to be accessing at all.

A dark moment grows even darker. Now a decision looms heavy in front of these students. Will they grasp all the more tightly to those beliefs they were sent off to campus with, and try all the more to claim them as their own? Or will they open their hands just enough for the stormy winds of the moment to blow away those light, hollow beliefs they once treasured? *Or* will they, right then and there, make the decision to not be caught with their beliefs in a state of unusable disarray ever again—at least to the extent they have any control over it—and therefore set out to learn and understand what they really believe about God, Jesus, the Holy Spirit, heaven and hell, sin and suffering, works and grace, and faith, hope and love?

Owned Faith

I was different from most of the kids I went to college with, or at least I thought I was. I chose to go to a Christian college not far from home. Having been a Christian for only a couple of years, and not feeling as if I had really *established* any beliefs beyond the basics—that Jesus loved me and saved me and was now working inside me to do something new—I felt like I was stepping onto a campus with peers who would have been classified as *theological giants* by comparison. It turned out that these peers of mine were not quite the theological giants I had assumed them to be; they were just further along on the journey than I was. Most of them did come from Christian homes, where they had learned *how* to pray, *why* to go to church, and the significance of serving others. Though I knew it wasn't a race, I felt light-years behind.

I can't tell you, with any great certainty, what it was that propelled me into a season of incredible interest, openness, and engagement of all things God, but what occurred over the course of my four years on campus can only be described as a spiritual explosion! As I searched for God and sought out new ways to grow in my faith, and put my beliefs into action, God seemed to be shaping me in inexplicable ways.

>> *We do not want to be beginners. But let us be convinced of the fact that we will never be anything else but beginners, all our life!*

— Thomas Merton, *Contemplative Prayer*[2]

The results of a transformed life—or better put, a transforming life—was not what I was after. I wanted to know God. I wanted to be close with Jesus and follow in His footsteps. I wanted to experience the richness and fullness of God's Spirit working inside me, and leading me, wherever that might take me. I wanted to love God, and others, well. As I pursued all of these things, God began to change me from the inside out. Transformation, or maybe a series of transformations, was taking place in my life. I was by no means perfect, or even as consistent as I might have hoped to have been, but the more I opened myself to God, the more I seemed to change.

I sought out every opportunity to worship, explore the Bible—alone and with others—and serve. I quickly learned the importance of living in intentional community with other followers of Jesus. I desired the kind of investment that Mentors could pour into me, as well as the kind of accountability and encouragement that a group of faithful friends could offer. I was, to a certain extent, OK with being the rookie Christian in the crowd I hung out with. My new friends seemed more than willing to extend extra measures of grace to me, as I was eager to *learn* and *know* and *live* as they did. I was like a sponge, soaking it all in. I couldn't get enough. I was in the process of owning my faith, choosing what I believed and how it was going to shape my life.

> > >

As I stated earlier, I'm not exactly sure what propelled me into such an extraordinary season of openness to God, or the transformation that occurred in my life, but I do know that I am not unique in this. Over the fifteen years I've been working with college students, I have seen countless students abandon themselves fully to God, and God's work in their lives, and transformed as a result of it. As amazing as it was to experience for myself, I often find it all the more amazing to watch it occur in the lives of students I work with. To see firsthand what God is doing, how students are responding, and the metamorphosis that seems to occur slowly—yet in the blink of an eye—is indescribable! I'm humbled each and every time. Because of my role as a pastor to college students, I also have the chance to see students whose faith seems to get stuck mid-journey. These students have taken some initial steps in making their faith their own but get to a place where they believe that they've arrived, that they've done enough. This is where a helpful *nudge* from someone like you can make a big difference in his or her life and development.

As with the family faith, the owned faith of students has its own set of positives and negatives. On the positive side, when a student transitions from their family faith to a more personal, owned faith, it represents a level of personal thought and decision that is incredibly significant (and we should help students to celebrate this!). It suggests that the student has deemed faith (1) worthy of some level of exploration, (2) worthy of keeping around in some form or fashion, and (3) worthy of making some personal commitments to. All of this represents a level of interest and openness to God and God's work in that student's life that is *quite* encouraging. It also has *the potential* to build further levels of commitment to, and confidence in, their faith. An owned faith shows all the potential of something significant, spectacular— even transformational—but it also has its own potential pitfalls.

An owned faith, for many students, can lead to a stagnating faith. The "work," they might tend to think, has been done and now they can move on to new ventures. But without an ongoing openness to, and passionate pursuit of, God on the part of the student, all of the investment in the world, from all of the most well-intentioned individuals, will not amount to much of anything. Why do I say this? Well, because I've seen this side of it too. An owned faith, when believed to be the end of the journey—and not the beginning of faith itself—can yield a number of negative attributes in the lives of young believers. For instance, they can begin to close themselves to faith conversations and exploration that might threaten to move them beyond the scope of their current set of beliefs. Students might also become content with a handful of beliefs that they believe to be "enough," even to the point of dismissing anything that pushes beyond the reaches of those beliefs. In fact, some of them may go so far as to proclaim that anyone—*anyone*—whose beliefs do not align with their own is simply misinformed and wrong. And just like that, they have reduced the body of Christ to a small percentage of believers who believe *exactly* as they do—and everyone else is considered to either be hellbound and/or a potential "convert."

>> *As students make decisions about what they believe, it shapes how they think and how they live.*

What does this look like on campus? Well, that depends on what kind of owned faith it is. As students make decisions about what they believe, it shapes how they think and how they live. The thing about an owned faith, however, is that it is often as static as the family faith that students once claimed ownership of. In many ways they've simply traded one static set of beliefs for another—that *they've* chosen—but that ultimately serves them only slightly better than the ones before did. Why? Because instead of holding on to it loosely, leaving room for it to grow and change and morph, these young believers cling to their *new* faith with a sort of herculean death grip. They've done the hard work of wading out into the murky waters of faith, leaving the safety of their family faith at the shoreline, and they've returned victorious with a new faith—an owned faith—in hand. Instead of placing this newly owned faith in the treasure box that their family faith once occupied, they place it upon the mantle over the proverbial fireplace of their lives, as a trophy of sorts. They have fought, and fought hard, for this faith, and now they can safely claim it as their own. The hard work has been done. They can check that off of their list and move on to the next thing. And if someone should ever ask them about that owned faith that sits upon the mantle, they can tell them—with all of the pride that only a true *owner* can put forth—all about it.

An owned faith, however, is not the end that many believe it to be. In fact, it may very well be the beginning of something incredibly dynamic and life changing. Still, many students will need the assistance of a Mentor-type to help them see this reality.

Growing Faith

During my senior year of college, I had the good fortune of living with six of my best guy friends. It was a fantastic way to end my college career , and I can recall several incredible conversations about life and faith and our futures. In some ways I felt as if I had finally "arrived," now being able "to keep pace" with my theologically advanced friends and classmates. I no longer felt like I had nothing to contribute to conversations about God and Jesus. My three-plus years at a Christian college had served me well, or so I thought. It was my friend Matt—yes, the same friend who introduced me to what it looked like to live a life of following Jesus—who now challenged the firm grip by which I was holding my faith.

"You can't do that, Guy!" he proclaimed.

"Why not?" I questioned.

"Because that's not how God works!" Matt shot back.

"I think it *is*," I insisted, "and therefore I'm just going to sit here and wait."

>> *As we travel on this path, the blessing of God will come upon us and reconstruct us into the image of Jesus Christ. We must always remember that the path does not produce the change; it only places us where the change can occur.*

— Richard Foster, Celebration of Discipline[3]

Matt was a good friend who was patiently trying to help me understand something that he had already learned: we will always attempt to put God in a box because it makes life easier. This once-interested-open-and-willing-to-engage-all-things God-believer (me) had learned some things, and in an attempt to better *manage* and *maximize* these things, I must have filed them nicely in my own little "God box." At that point in time I had apparently come to the conclusion that it was OK to sit still, and literally do nothing, while waiting for God to tell me what I was supposed to do next. Matt was insistent that while God *can* work that way He rarely does. Instead, he suggested that God was much more interested in figuring things out with me. It wasn't so much about the destination as it was about the journey we would be on, together, that would make arriving at the destination—regardless of wherever it might be—so significant. I, however, was having a difficult time hearing him because I had become firmly set in my belief that I could just sit and wait, believing that God would provide Divine handwriting on the wall.

I don't believe that anymore, but I did for a while, and I think a lot of young-in-their-faith believers do at some point. I'm not sure why I believed what I did, or where that belief came from, but I know I liked it—and I didn't like Matt messing with it. It may not have been until sometime during my first year *after* college, while reading Richard Foster's *Celebration of Discipline* for the first time, that I came to better understand what it meant to have a *dynamic* relationship with God—and what, exactly, my friend Matt was trying to help me understand. The ways we actively engage our faith, and attempt to live it out, are like being a part of a Divine dance—one where God takes the lead and we follow, one where we don't have the option to sit out but are ultimately an *active* and necessary participant in what is taking place.

> > >

You don't have to think about this long to see the grace and beauty of being invited into such an experience—a process of working with God, in an ongoing fashion, to become the men and women of faith that we were created to be. If you sit with that reality a little longer though, the enormity and weight of it will likely start to make itself known, and attempt to scare you off. You see, we like things neat, easy, and predictable. And so do students. We like things black and white. It's easier that way. We have two choices—one of them right, the other wrong—and we're simply given the opportunity to choose. That seems easy enough. And we want God to work that way. We want God to give us clear-cut choices. Better yet, we want God to simply do all of the work for us—to show the options and to show which one is best—and make sure that we know why! And so do students. But if God's not going to do all of the work, most students prefer that they be given full control to do all of the

Spiritual formation is not an option! The inescapable conclusion is that life itself is a process of spiritual development. The only choice we have is whether that growth moves us toward wholeness in Christ or toward an increasingly dehumanized and destructive mode of being.

— Robert Mulholland, *Invitation to a Journey*[4]

work. It works better that way, they think—either it's all God or it's all them. But it most certainly cannot fall somewhere between these two options because that's just too difficult to conceive of.

But that, by definition, is what a *growing faith* is. It's this ever-morphing, always-changing thing that involves God's work *and* our work. It's rarely work that is divided down the middle—50 percent God and 50 percent us. It often feels like we're doing the majority of the work, when in reality it is almost always God who is doing the majority of the work. It's never complete but always a work-in-progress. It can never be shelved, or boxed. It must be continually interacted with. It's dynamic and therefore always *growing* and changing because it is never given the chance to just sit there, unengaged. I'm no dancer, but I do know enough to know that it takes two *equally* committed, engaged partners to make a dance look like something beautiful and not awkward. It takes a leader and a follower. Both play significant roles, yet there's no confusion about who is dictating the pace, the steps, the timing, and the overall direction of the dance.

A growing faith has a number of positives and no real negatives. I say no *real* negatives because I think there will be those of us who struggle with the fact that it's always changing, which means that it requires constant attention and engagement. The challenge—and perceived negative for some of us (maybe students especially)—is there is never a chance to check it off of a list. For those of us who are wired to organize things into "manageable" tasks, give it the necessary time and attention, and eventually mark it off as "complete," well, there's no chance to do so with a growing faith. Our faith is not meant to be seen as something to be "completed." It's meant to be forever a work in progress. And this will drive some students nuts!

But if we can get students beyond that, there are some incredible benefits to having a growing faith. First, students in this place are always growing—even when it doesn't feel like they are—because as they pursue Christ and find ways to stretch their faith and put it into action, God will continue to change them! This growing faith also will lend itself to one being much more open to, and accepting of, people who believe different from they do. As they enter into conversations and experiences that expose them to new ways of thinking and believing, God will both grow them and use them. In this way, they will have taken the hand-cuffs of an owned faith off of God and drastically increased the ways in which He can use and shape them.

What does a growing faith look like on campus? Well, it's both bold *and* attractive. The young believer is not ashamed of what they believe but go about their living with a confidence that comes in knowing both *who* they are and *Whose* they are. It's approachable and accepting. Unlike the owned faith that tends to keep to itself and point the finger of judgment at those who are different; those with a growing faith invite others into conversations and relationships—willing to accept the other as they are. It's passionate and congruent. What the believer says, and how they live their life, matches up. It's *not* perfect, but it is much infused with the Holy Spirit and bears a growing likeness to Jesus.

《

Therefore everyone who hears these words of mine and puts them into practice is like a wise man who built his house on the rock. The rain came down, the streams rose, and the winds blew and beat against that house; yet it did not fall, because it had its foundation on the rock. But everyone who hears these words of mine and does not put them into practice is like a foolish man who built his house on sand. The rain came down, the streams rose, and the winds blew and beat against that house, and it fell with a great crash.

— Jesus, Matthew 7:24-27

Why It Matters

Faith is one of several areas of life that should be both consistent and ever changing. The college years provide some of the most fertile soil for growth and maturation in our faith. And regardless of whether or not students believe it to be cool to love Jesus or give priority to faith-forming activities or get up for church on Sunday mornings or live as if Jesus is serious about what He says He wants from those who choose to follow Him, there is no more important question than what do we think about Jesus—what do we believe about Jesus—and how, then, will that inform how we live? For college students, this must serve as the foundation on which everything else is built. It must serve as the lens through which everything else is both viewed *and* understood. Young believers *must* take this part of their story seriously—or they cannot expect the rest of the journey to make much sense.

THE MENTOR'S TOOLBOX

- How are you assisting students in this process of moving from a *family faith* to an *owned faith* to a *growing faith*? What are you modeling for students in this regard?
- What role do you think you should be playing in this process? Why?
- What difference do you think it will make for students to have their relationship with God as the foundation on which they build their college experience? Why?

Take some time to reflect on these questions in the space provided on the following page.

Here are several questions that might help to promote conversation with your student in this area:
- How would you classify the current state of your spiritual life? Why?
- What do you think it's going to take to move forward on your personal faith journey? Who might be able to help you best during this season of your journey?
- What difference do you think it will make to have your relationship with God as the foundation on which you base all other decisions during your college years? Why?

For further reading on the subject of faith formation, consider:
- *Stages of Faith* by James Fowler
- *Celebration of Discipline* by Richard Foster
- *Invitation to a Journey* by Robert Mulholland

Notes, questions, reminders,
points of action, etc.

4
Life Lens

Inherited Worldview » Biblical Worldview »
Integrated Worldview

Do not conform to the pattern of this world,
but be transformed by the renewing of your mind.
Then you will be able to test and approve what God's will is—
his good, pleasing and perfect will.
— Romans 12:2

When I was a child, I talked like a child,
I thought like a child, I reasoned like a child.
When I became a man,
I put the ways of childhood behind me.
— 1 Corinthians 13:11

B y the time students arrive on campus, most of them have been *trained* (in some form or fashion), for the better part of eighteen years, on how to view the world. They have been given a lens, which has been constructed by someone else, through which to view (and understand) the world. Maybe it was their parents or grandparents, a pastor or family friend. Regardless, it is likely that the student did little, if anything, to help construct the lens through which they view the world around them. This means that the ways they've been taught to view, interpret, and understand things like war, politics, religion, education, life, death, marriage, divorce, sex, relationships, money, poverty, work, children, community, independence, dependence, diversity, equality, race, gender, sexuality, government, and on and on was likely not of their own choosing. And it's not that it was forced upon them either. The adults in their world—with all of their own issues, irregularities, and imperfections—sought to instill in them the ways of thinking and living that made the most sense to them. For better, or for worse, they have fitted their students with a lens that *they* now must examine and make some decisions about.

But why?

Well, because a lot hinges upon this lens through which they view, interpret, and understand life.

Again, the adults who collectively crafted and affixed this lens to their student—no matter how well-intentioned they were—were imperfect. As a student begins to more closely examine the lens, parts of it likely will remain because they work and they feel right to the student. But other parts, after some poking and prodding, will prove to be more of a hindrance than a help. These elements will need to be thought through, and our students will need to make some decisions about what will replace the elements from their lens that were removed. *This is an important process* and will likely take some time, thoughtful examination, and reflection, as well as intentional decision making on the part of our students. And while students can choose to delay this important developmental process by putting it off until later in life, it is a mistake.

I've said it before, and I'll say it again here: the college years are some of the most formative in life! To put off something as important as the construction of a life lens—one that helps them to view, interpret, and understand all that is happening during these formative years—is a colossal mistake.

So, let's begin to explore the process of developing a life lens that starts where students are and ends with a way of viewing, interpreting, and understanding the world around them that, at the very least, is of their own making.

Inherited Worldview

When I went off to college there was a lot I didn't know, and a lot more that I didn't realize I didn't know, both about myself and the world in which I lived.

I grew up in quite a loving home. Both my parents expressed their love for me and my brothers on a regular basis in their own unique ways. They also showed a lot of affection toward one another. PDA (or personal displays of affection), especially within the home, was commonplace.

My mother, in particular, seemed to be filled with endless amounts of love for my dad, brothers, and me. She often stressed the importance of family, of being kind to one another, of taking time to simply be together. I don't know that I valued it as much at the time, but it definitely left an impression on me, and all the more as I grew up and learned more about the tough home life she grew up in.

Likewise, my dad experienced some challenging things at home during his growing-up years. His dad was an alcoholic—something he brought home with him from his years of serving in the army. To make matters worse, my dad's tender and loving mom passed away when he was only sixteen, after losing her fight with cancer.

This pair would have been given quite poor odds in Vegas, but somehow they seemed to overcome those odds and provide a family environment—filled with so much love—that was drastically different from the one they each grew up in.

Spiritually speaking, the home my parents made for our family was, among other things, nominally Christian. We went to church on Sunday mornings, but that was it. We didn't pray at meals, read the Bible, or talk about God, heaven, hell or why any of it mattered. I think my parents would say that it was never made to be all that important in their childhood homes, which speaks to why our home was shaped the way it was during my growing-up years. It wasn't until my parents had me and my brothers that they decided maybe it was time to think about getting plugged in to a church. Apparently raising kids revealed a need that could not be met solely within our home so my parents set off into unfamiliar territory and eventually found a well-attended Lutheran church for us to become a part of. We became a family of Lutherans and went to church most Sundays, so that we could then go out to breakfast with our extended family—more seemingly nominal Christians.

My extended family played a big role in my life during my growing-up years. For much of my first eighteen years, my parents' siblings and parents (who were alive) lived within a fifteen-minute drive. We saw them regularly. I remember liking this. And as all families do, ours had its fair share of issues. Within the few generations immediately present on both sides of the family, we encountered alcoholism, verbal abuse, depression, divorce, illness, drugs, imprisonment, unemployment, relocation, stress, tension between parents and grandparents, tension between parents and kids, and so on. Much of it was not talked about openly. A lot of what I knew was because I happened to overhear enough of one side of a phone conversation to be able to piece some things together, or because I was within earshot of discussions happening between adult relatives when they didn't think any of us kids were paying attention. Between the issues, and the ways in which our extended family dealt with these issues (or didn't deal with them), impressions were made.

Equally impressionistic was the work ethic I saw my parents live out. They worked hard. At work. At home. They did whatever was necessary to provide a nice and clean home, food, clothing, and opportunities to do lots of fun stuff. My dad regularly came home from a day at the office, changed clothes, and maybe sat for a few minutes before heading outside to work on something—the car, the yard, cleaning out the garage, or putting a fresh coat of paint on the house or the deck or the railroad ties that outlined much of the landscape throughout our yard. Not to be outdone, my mom seemed to keep the house impeccably clean. Laundry was in a constant state of wash, dry, fold, return to rooms, repeat. Home-cooked meals, lots of cookies, and a desire to keep all of her boys well-fed seemed to be a well-deserved badge of honor that she proudly wore. While my arm often had to be twisted in order to pitch in, and do my fair share around the house, their tireless work ethic left an impression on me.

Money was an issue, I think. Again, nothing was ever really talked about openly. My parents rarely seemed to disagree about things, but every now and again they could be caught trying to calmly discuss the nature of different purchases or the size of the grocery bill or the true need to outfit each of us kids for the new school year or the cost of having multiple boys involved in multiple activities throughout the course of the year. And while I don't think we were ever lavished upon, at least according to some standards, I don't believe I was ever without anything I needed. Of course, this didn't account for all of the things I *wanted*, and was not given, which opened the door for me to start working as teenager. My parents traveled, and we traveled as a family—not as much as some but definitely more than others. We weren't rich; in fact, my dad would probably scoff at such a suggestion. I probably had more than my fair share growing up. And it shaped me.

Oh, and in case you hadn't picked up on it, communication was a bit of an issue as well! All the previous mentions of how things were "never talked about openly" were indicative of how my family dealt with issues. If, and I do stress *if* (from my perspective as a child), things were dealt with in our home, it typically happened out of the earshot of us kids. My parents, I found out along my growing-up years, both came from homes where a lot of discord and yelling occurred. So the fact that I remember my parents rarely fighting makes sense—by rarely I mean less than a handful of times. It made for quite a peaceful home growing up. I don't know how healthy we were, but we seemed to be at peace. I don't know how anything ever got resolved—I assume it did— but you know what they say about assuming.

Beyond that, I don't recall ever hearing much about politics in our home, or in the homes of extended family and friends for that matter. My parents were adamant about my education, but other than the daily newspaper, I don't recall them being big readers themselves. I know my dad had graduated from college, after coming out of the army, and that my mom often lamented about starting but not finishing (at least not finishing until recently). My parents wanted good things for my brothers and me to the extent that they were willing to make sacrifices—far more than I'm sure I ever realized at the time, or even now. All of this, I'm quite certain, shaped me.

> > >

Much like an inherited faith, as mentioned in the previous chapter, an inherited worldview is where most of our students naturally start as young women and men who are just beginning college. For much of their lives they were exposed to influences,

So where do we get our worldview?

*We would like to think we got it on our own.
That we assembled and examined all
the evidence and chose the worldview that was
the most defensible or "right," then proceeded
to use that worldview as our assumption for
explaining things. Sorry. Most of us inherited our
worldview. We got it from our family, friends,
the media and the experiences of life.*

— Keith Drury, paper presented, Fall Religion Colloquium[1]

images, practices, and people that served to shape the way that they view, interpret, and understand the world. It didn't happen all at once, but starting at the moment they entered the world, they began to be shaped and molded by everything they encountered. As infants they quickly learned who loved them and met the majority of their needs. As toddlers they were prompted to learn how to walk—by influences young and old—in order that they might keep up with, or get out of the way of, those moving all around them. Simultaneously they were learning to talk; it started with grunts and squeaks and giggles and squeals before eventually turning into words and phrases and sentences and conversations. Life went on and so did their development. Motor skills, emotional intelligence, social capacities, mental cognition, and a developing worldview were all a part of their growing-up process. The years that made up their lives before heading off to college included a number of influences. From friends to teachers and coaches, pastors and youth pastors, and parents and grandparents, all have played a role in helping students to become who they are today, as well as to shape their worldviews. And it was likely those who were more passionate about one thing or another (religion or politics, knowledge and the academy, or personal experience and the exploration of freedoms and boundaries) who left more lasting impressions on a student and served to shape them in more sizeable ways. These people and experiences shaped what students liked and what they didn't like. They shaped what students prioritized. They shaped what they valued. They shaped what they feared.

And while our students' friends proved to have a profound impact on some of their *immediate* choices in life—and specific teachers and/or coaches were there to speak into their lives at critical moments—it was, and likely still is, their family of origin who has provided them with the vast majority of material that has served to organically construct their current life lens.

Think about that for a minute. Consider a belief or a practice of your own—something that holds significant meaning in your life, something that makes you, you. Now, can you identify why it holds such meaning for you? Can you recall who has influenced this in your life? Let's go back further. Do you remember who introduced you to this idea or belief or practice? Do you know why they introduced it to you? Do you know what meaning it holds in *their* life? And how much of your current understanding of this idea, belief, or practice resembles what it first did when it was first introduced to you? How much of it has changed since then? Why has it changed? Who or what has influenced the changes?

Now, do you think *that* idea, belief, or practice would be as significant in your life today without the influence of the person(s) or experience(s) that you just identified? How might your life be different had *that* idea, belief, or practice never been introduced to your life? How might your life be different had the *different people or events* that have served to shape that idea, belief, or practice not been a part of your life? And when you stop to consider this is only *one* idea, belief, or practice that we've explored—among *hundreds*, if not *thousands*—that make up how you see, interpret, understand, and live in the world, you quickly begin to see how great and how vast are the influences that have shaped *you,* as well as your students.

An inherited life lens is a starting point. Some will be better than others, but each will serve as a starting point nonetheless. A part of our task, our journey with students, is to help them begin to explore their life lens and recognize the need to make some intentional decisions about it. What about it is helpful? What's harmful? Some of this will be difficult to comprehend depending on the extent to which the Bible is serving to shape this conversation, and ultimate life lens.

Biblical Worldview

In 2007, A. J. Jacobs wrote a book entitled *A Year of Living Biblically: One Man's Humble Attempt to Follow the Bible as Literally as Possible.* For a full year this man attempted to live according to a way of life he found described and defined in the Bible. From not cutting his beard to loving his neighbor, Jacobs sought to live out the laws and lifestyles (both big and small) set forth by God in the Bible.

And while this may sound extreme, on one hand, it should make sense to us, at least to some degree, on the other.

Isn't that what we're called to as Christians? A way of living that is different (drastically so, in many cases) from the world in which we live? Jacobs is not the first to consider such a lifestyle. Many even today believe that God has set for us a way of living (as found in the Bible) we as Christians are supposed to embody.

Consider present-day monks and nuns. It's a way of life that many cannot comprehend. Vows of chastity and purity. Vows of celibacy and silence. Communal living and a vow of intentional poverty. Yes, it's a lifestyle that describes quite an intentional move away from the American pace of life, and ways of living, that many of us would struggle to fully embrace. It's an intentional move away from "this world" and toward a simpler, less distracting, and more heavenly-minded way of life in this world. It's a way of living that more closely resembles the way of life God seems to call His followers to.

But why would someone (anyone) choose this way of life today? Can't we live faithful lives without withdrawing from the culture and committing ourselves to such extreme measures? Sure. But with the noise and clutter of our American culture come a lot of distractions and deterrents from following closely the ways of Jesus.

>> *The percentage of Americans taking a literal view of the Bible has declined over time, from an average of 38% from 1976-1984 to an average of 31% since. However, highly religious Americans— particularly those of Protestant faiths—still commonly believe in a literal interpretation of the Bible.*

— www.gallup.com²

As we begin to read the Bible, early on we learn that God created this world (and all that is within it)—and it was good. God had established an existence in the garden of Eden where Adam and Eve were able to walk and talk with God. Adam and Eve were naked, before each other and God, and not ashamed. Life was perfect. Life was right. Life was as God intended it to be.

And then, in Genesis chapter 3, we see that Adam and Eve decided to go against a request—a command—that God had made to not eat from the tree of the knowledge of good and evil. When they did eat the fruit of this tree, there was an awareness—a way of seeing and understanding the world—that wasn't there before. They had a *lens* that was not intended for them. And as a result, there was separation from God.

God's creation ceased to be as He wanted it to be. And many say that ever since then humankind has been slowly (or in some instances, speedily) spiraling downward. It's true we live in a broken world, with broken people, and some believe that the best thing to do is to retreat from the evils of the world to "safe havens" where well-intentioned, faithful believers can attempt to live in God's ways, without all of the evil and distractions present in our culture.

For them, it has become a black-and-white existence.

God, and the things of God, are good. Everything else is bad—evil. The only way to "be faithful" to God is to withdraw from the world, to shun everything that doesn't ooze of God. If this means drastically restricting the things they do, consume, or relate to, then that's what they do.

OK, I'll confess that I've wandered down a bit of an extremist path, but the reality is, in an attempt to live with a biblical worldview, many people have a difficult time not thinking in black-and-white terms. It's easier that way. When things are black or white, they're easier to distinguish between. But when people start talking about "shades of gray," life (and faith, and a way of biblically viewing the world) becomes a lot more challenging. Most of us don't like challenging so if everything can be categorized in simple, black-and-white terms, life will be more easily managed and maneuvered.

> > >

I can't recall where I first heard the term "biblical worldview," but I'm quite sure my early understanding of it was both confused and convoluted. I think this is, in part, because many of the people I hear using the term today have quite a negative view of the world in which we live. Many of them share the belief that humans have messed up what God had created. While there is definitely some truth to that statement, I think it paints an incomplete picture of the greater story.

Most of us have not been taught how to view and understand the world through the lens of the Bible. It's a part of living with a compartmentalized faith. We access the biblical text when at church or engaging in Bible study but don't give it much consideration when it comes to day-to-day living.

And the same is true of students.

This issue of learning to experience life through the lens of the Bible ties back in to the question of relevance that we explored in chapter 3.1. And a significant part of moving faith from irrelevant to peripheral to central is allowing faith to shape the way we see and understand the world and all of its events.

As someone who has likely gone through this process yourself, you know how challenging this can be. Our first attempts at getting into the Bible are challenging enough themselves, but then to further attempt to use it as a lens through which to begin to interpret, comprehend, and even discern the happenings in our world is a sizeable task. Yet for many new believers, it is a switch that makes a lot of sense.

*Up to this point I've spent my entire life living a certain way—the world's way—*a new believer might rationalize, *and it's not been working. And Jesus has now come in and changed my life, which must mean that He wants to change the way I live and move and have my being.* They take seriously Paul's charge: "Do not conform to the pattern of this world, but be transformed by the renewing of your mind. Then you will be able to test and approve what God's will is—his good, pleasing and perfect will" (Romans 12:2).

And as they do this they begin to change, quite radically. They flip the switch. They go from black to white.

They find themselves in tension with many of the ways in which they've been thinking and living. And they don't like living in tension. It's uncomfortable. Breaking their faith out of the silo it's been in, they give it free reign in their lives. They see the need for major change(s) in their lives, and they make them in sweeping fashion. Whatever the Bible says, that's what they do— no matter how far a departure it is from their old ways of being. In many instances they will be unrecognizable to those to whom they are closest. It changes their priorities, their patterns, and even their personality. They find themselves associating closely with God and His mission in the world, and can become fanatical (in extreme instances) in this new way of living for Christ.

They are quite certain that this new way of life honors God, but does it?

They have classified the world—God's Creation—as bad and have systematically cut themselves off from everything within it that doesn't honor or glorify God.

But how does that speak to redemption? Restoration?

How does that show an understanding of how God might want to use His followers in this world to bring about change? To help restore God's creation toward what it once was? To offer peace in the midst of chaos and love in the midst of pain and hope to a hurting world.

So if an inherited worldview offers us one way of understanding the world (one that is often more cultural in nature), then a biblical worldview offers us something that is drastically different. And I tend to believe that we actually need to hold these two (seemingly opposing worldviews) together, in tension, to get an even better understanding of what God is up to in the world and how He might desire to use us in this place.

> *A person with a biblical worldview experiences, interprets, and responds to reality in light of the Bible's principles. What Scripture teaches is the primary grid for making decisions and interacting with the world.*
> — David Kinnaman, *UnChristian*[3]

Integrated Worldview

I recently learned of a guy here in Nashville who's doing an amazing work. He's offering, free of charge, counseling services for people in the music industry. He's reaching out to a unique community and offering them the kind of personal assistance that most think they don't need (because they're "living the dream"), and even if they did, they could totally pay for (because everyone in the music business is rich—not true). Did I mention he's doing this free of charge?!

And if that wasn't noble enough, he's recently struck out on a new adventure, looking to help more people in the world. He decided he wanted to become a philanthropist but then realized he didn't have any money, and it's hard to be a philanthropist if you don't have money. So rather than start charging all of the good folks who were taking him up on his offer for free counseling, he decided he'd raise money that he could then give away.

So he wrote a children's book—with the help of about a dozen other people who heard about his idea and decided to offer their own unique skills and creative gifts to the process and project. And while the book was in the process of being developed, he reached out to ten different nonprofits here in our community to see how they could benefit from a significant donation to their organization. The one I heard about was Thistle Farms and the women of Magdalene House.

If you're unfamiliar with this organization, and these women, here's the short of it. The Magdalene House is a collection of four homes here in Nashville that serves as a halfway house for homeless women and former prostitutes who are trying to get back on their feet. Thistle Farms is a place where these women work, making bath and body products, in order to earn a wage and gain important job experience. They are a subsection of our population that most have written off, including many Christians. *They have chosen a destructive way of life and are now reaping the consequences of their own choices*, we might argue. *They've made their beds; now let them lie in them.* They are seen as unredeemable to many, maybe most.

Not, however, to those who started this unique ministry. And not to Bob, the guy with the book idea, who's now using his children's book to raise money to help pay for a product elevator in the Thistle Farms work space. You see, many of these women, because of things their bodies have had to endure, struggle to move the products from the production floor to the space where they are packaged. This might not seem like a big deal, but to this ministry—and these women— it is. A product elevator would make a world of difference to these women and the work they do. And this is only one of the ways that Bob is hoping to help bring about change in a world in need. He's choosing to make a difference—to help usher in God's kingdom—in some very practical ways.

Take your Bible and take your newspaper, and read both. But interpret newspapers from your Bible.

— Karl Barth[4]

There are a growing number of ministries like this out there. You've possibly heard of organizations like TOMS shoes and Blood Water Mission and others similar to them. They were started by people whose faith implicated them in a hurting world. It made them want to be a part of a solution, instead of pretending as if the problem didn't exist. They want to be used by God to make all things new. They want to be a part of the redemption and restoration process.

And this kind of meaningful life is something that is getting the attention of many of our students. They want to live lives of meaning and purpose, but many struggle to connect the dots between their faith and this process, between making money and making a difference.

> > >

Living in tension is difficult.

Learning to get used to living in tension is even harder, but I think that's exactly what we're called, as followers of Jesus, to do.

I once heard author Leonard Sweet suggest that as believers we should walk through the world with a Bible in one hand and a newspaper in the other (I imagine that nowadays he would suggest something like a news stream on a handheld device, in order to be more current). Sweet was tapping into the words and beliefs of evangelist Billy Graham, and theologian Karl Barth before him. It's the practice of overlaying two different lenses—or ways of viewing, interpreting, and understanding the world—and using them together. We use both to help us understand what's going on, and how it is that God might want us to respond.

We don't run from the world, but we don't fully embrace it (as it is) either. We're called to live a now-but-not-yet kind of existence.

We're called to live in a place of tension within the world that allows us to see things as they really are—the way that God sees them—and then move in response to God's leading, in order to help bring about meaningful change. It involves being more than aware of what's going on in the world; it involves actually caring about it. It means consciously choosing to be a part of the solution, rather than only lamenting about all of the problems.

It involves having hope instead of despair.

Choosing to see the world as it could be instead of what it currently is or is not.

It means being open and available to being used by God to help bring about His redemptive work—*Thy kingdom come, on earth as it is in heaven.*

And this is an important process to begin during the formative college years. As our students begin to engage their faith in ways that suggest they better understand what's going on in the world, and how best to engage it, then we are able to begin to address more some specific areas of the college experience that—through the lens of faith—can make all the difference in the world.

THE MENTOR'S TOOLBOX

- How has this chapter caused you to (re)consider your own way(s) of thinking about, and living in, the world?
- How have you (or are you) growing in your ability to "live in tension" in this world, such that you see the world for what it "could be" and see yourself as an agent of change and redemption that God can use to help make "all things new"?
- What are the ways in which this is still a struggle for you?
- How can you be open and honest with your student(s) regarding your own development in this area?
- What are some ways you need to further surrender to (or better work with) God in this area of your life?

Take some time to reflect on these questions in the space provided on the following page.

Here are several questions that might help to promote conversation with your student in this area:

- How do you understand God and the world?
- How do you understand God's present role and work in the world?
- What most frustrates you about the world? About God's role in the world?
- How does your faith impact your understanding of what's happening in the world?
- As a Christian, do you feel any kind of tension living in the world? If so, how would you describe it? What do you think is the source of that tension? Do you think it's a tension that can be (or should be) resolved?

For further reading on the subject of worldview, consider:

- *Christ and Culture* by H. Richard Niebuhr
- *A Primer on Postmodernism* by Stanley J. Grenz

Notes, questions, reminders,
points of action, etc.

5
College

The Next (Best) Thing » "My" Career »
Preparing to Fulfill God's Call

"For I know the plans I have for you," declares the LORD,
"plans to prosper you and not to harm you,
plans to give you hope and a future."
— Jeremiah 29:11

He has shown you, O mortal, what is good.
And what does the LORD require of you?
To act justly and to love mercy
and to walk humbly with your God.
— Micah 6:8 NIV

've been connected with university life for most of the past twenty years. I graduated from my own undergraduate experience back in the spring of 1997. In the fifteen years of my working life since then, I have spent all but six months on college campuses. I don't want to overestimate my level of expertise in the area of student life, within higher education; but over the course of my own education, work experience, and personal observation I've seen an increasing percentage of students fail to make the most of their formative college years. More and more students are showing up on campus with little to no clue as to why they are there and spending some of the most formative years of their life floundering about—with no real direction or sense of purpose.

College is supposed be a time of growth and maturation—a time of transitioning from youth to adulthood—or at the very least an honest attempt at starting that process. But the truth is that it seems to be occurring less and less. A growing percentage of students are going to college simply because it's expected of them. For the majority of the students we see on American college and university campuses, pursuing a college degree was a foregone conclusion since the day they were conceived. Not too long ago, college was a strategic choice made by high school graduates who *knew* they needed the kind of specialized education that a college degree would afford them, in order to get the kind of job they *knew* they desired.

Now you might be thinking to yourself, Isn't this still true today? Don't college students still need to get a specialized education in order to be prepared and considered "marketable" out in the working world? And I think we can safely say that, yes, students need the kind of education pursuing a college degree is meant to provide. In fact, all the more so today.

But the reality is, most students *don't* know what they want to do with their lives. They don't know why they're pursuing a college degree, other than that it's expected of them (and likely, what they've come to expect of themselves). They don't know how it will benefit their futures, other than that it should keep them from having to work a minimum-wage job. They likely won't take too seriously the pursuit of their degree because they don't know how (or if) it will ever be necessary in their lives (that's what a master's degree is for, or so it has come to be for an increasing percentage of college graduates). With no clear sense of calling or purpose, many students will incur a lot of debt while pursuing degrees that they will not (or cannot) use.

College, simply put, is only the next expected thing. It's like the thirteenth grade.

A part of our task as Mentors is to come alongside these emerging adults and help them begin to evolve in their understanding of what college is really all about. From the next best thing to thinking about college as a place to be prepared for their career is an important and natural step. But the often-unconsidered next step beyond personal career is thinking about how God might want to use this educational opportunity to prepare them to make a difference in the world. It's a transition from thinking about a personal payday to how they can work with God to make the world a better place, and how God might need to use their formative college years to better prepare them for this important work.

But students won't make it to this place of understanding college on their own. They'll need your help.

> *In the 1970s, a person with a bachelor's degree earned 25% more than a person without one. Today's college graduate earns 60% more. People without a college degree earn 31% less in inflation-adjusted dollars than they did just 20 years ago.*
> — www.huffingtonpost.com[1]

The Next (Best) Thing

As I think back to my own early inclinations about college I truthfully can't remember a whole lot. I can't ever remember making a conscious decision to attend college. I don't remember having any conversations with my parents about this, at least none that I remember initiating. I don't think there was ever a doubt in my mind that I would attend college; it was more of a foregone conclusion. The only question on the table must have been *where* to attend when it was finally time.

>> *Nearly 2 in 25 people age 25 and over have a master's, about the same proportion that had a bachelor's or higher in 1960.*
> — www.nytimes.com[2]

My first real memory of exploring my options for college came as a part of a visit I made (as a senior in high school) to a nearby campus to visit a friend of mine who was attending there. It was a private Christian school, and as a relatively new Christian at that point in time, I can only remember the feeling I had when I was on campus for that unofficial visit. I didn't know anything about the school or its reputation, the academic programs that were offered, the quality of the education, or even what I would study. But the campus seemed to "ooze" Jesus. So, as a relatively new Christian, that was enough to convince me that this was the school for me.

As you might imagine, this was exposed as a flimsy rationale for making such a significant choice, especially to my fiscally minded parents (my dad in particular). I think they had long assumed that I would attend the local state university. So my desire to attend this (much more) expensive *Christian* university caught them more than a little off guard. But after talking through some of the finances, and agreeing to pay my fair share of it (I had no clue what I was signing on to at the time), they agreed to let me pursue it.

It was the *only* school I applied to.

And I got in.

I had no idea what I wanted to do with my life, but I knew I wanted to spend the next four years at *that* school, while I waited on God to help me figure out the rest.

Wanting to appear as though I had some clue as to why I was going to pay so much money for my education—and maybe to appease my parents, to some extent, I *did* declare myself as a science major upon entering my freshman year. To my credit, it was an area I had excelled in during high school, but I still didn't see how that was going to lead to anything I wanted to do with my life. Truth be told, I'm quite sure I didn't care. I just wanted to have that "life-changing" decision out of the way.

> > >

For most eighteen-year-olds today in the U.S., college is not just an option but truthfully the expected "next step" after high school graduation. And because most high-schoolers are without reason to question the logic, or purpose, of this, they set out to find the *perfect* school for themselves. Having engaged in little vocational discernment, if any, their selection is often guided by a number of factors but none relating to how God might want to prepare them to do good work in the world.

Once they've made their choice, and arrived at their dream school, how do they spend their unfocused year(s)? Well, according to Tim Clydesdale's book, *The First Year Out*, these students are primarily interested in (and focused on) connecting socially, pursuing intimacy, and learning how to manage their lives—making friends; desiring intimacy with someone special; and learning how to manage their time, finances, and decision making. It says nothing of academic rigor; exploring their gifts, talents or passions; or even trying to achieve good academic standing. No, students are interested in making new friends, searching for someone special, and figuring out how to live as comfortably as they can, given their new context. Finally being out on their own, most college students seem to need time and space to learn some of the basics of life. They've left the protective wing of the family nest and are having to learn how to navigate the big, big world on their own. The learning curve seems to be growing, but college is an expensive location for this kind of education. And left alone, many college students could spend much of their college career working toward mastering some of these basic life skills. But we know that there's so much more available to them in this context. The college years are pregnant with potential!

>> *Today, full-time college students on average report spending only twenty-seven hours per week on academic activities—that is, less time than a typical high school student spends at school. Average time studying fell from twenty-five hours per week in 1961 to twenty hours per week in 1981 and thirteen hours per week in 2003.*

— Richard Arum and Josipa Roksa, *Academically Adrift*[3]

And so, as Mentors, we're called to action. Called to come alongside our students and help them begin to explore why they are there. To help them start thinking about life after college, what they might want to do, and how these years might help them to figure some of that out. Regardless of what got them to campus, once there, it's our responsibility to begin to engage them in such a way that their eyes are opened to the potential these years hold for preparing them for lives of meaningful work. We need to challenge them to step into (here it comes again) *responsibility* and consider how to best utilize the incredible academic opportunities they've been afforded.

"My" Career

As I mentioned early in this chapter, I went off to college with (the appearance of) a plan. I was going to be a science major. Not any old science major though, I was going to be a *marine biologist*. Doesn't that sound awesome!? I thought so. I was going to work with dolphins down somewhere off the coast of the Florida Keys. This, of course, made my decision to attend this private Christian school—nestled nicely in the suburbs of the Twin Cities in Minnesota—all the more practical. I hadn't yet figured out how (or when, or even if) a move to a more tropical location and school might be necessary, but for some reason I was quite certain that my future plans entailed living in a warm and sunny environment and playing with sea creatures (in between catching waves and taking naps on the beach).

> *Statistics show that college graduation correlates positively with economic factors like lower rates of unemployment and higher earnings.*
>
> — Holly Epstein Ojalva, *Why Go to College at All?*[4]

My plans were solidifying—until I got my grades back after my first semester. Turns out my late-night, social life and early-morning job as a lifeguard at a nearby pool did *not* set me up well for my midmorning General Biology 1 class (in a warm, dimly-lit room). Thinking with a bit more of intention about my high school science career, it turns out I was actually a lot better at physics and chemistry than I was biology. So that, plus the only *D* of my college career, helped to get me thinking toward a different kind of future in the sciences.

So as I returned to campus after my first extended Christmas break, I decided to hone in on chemistry. I couldn't tell you why—now or then—because although I knew I had a mind that understood chemistry, I could not foresee myself working in a lab or teaching it in a class—which were the only two things I believed someone with a chemistry degree was qualified to do. Am I proving the need to have this line of conversation with students?

I wasn't motivated by wealth or fortune—or maybe I should say that I wasn't obsessed with it. I'm sure I was thinking about a comfortable future, by North American standards, so money *was* a factor. But I wasn't out to make millions. I just wanted to be able to afford the things that I wanted to be able to afford. My own version of the "American Dream."

> > >

At some point during their college years, most students will find their way to an understanding about what they want to do with their lives (i.e., a job they think they can see themselves working in after they graduate from college). A number of motivating factors exist, but more than any other (or possibly, all of the others combined) the decision is most often based on potential future earnings.

Money.

The bottom line.

I have to believe that for most parents, who are likely helping to foot the bill for their child's college experience, the idea of a payoff—at the end of all of the money they've paid out—has to give the appearance of being on track. In fact, it's how the American Dream starts off: a good degree leads to a well-paying job, which leads to a loving spouse, two-and-half kids, a dog, and a comfortable lifestyle. From there it's about the pursuit of better, even higher-paying jobs that can yield more disposable income—and greater, more extravagant comforts. Everything becomes about accumulation, consumption, and comfort.

Everything is centered on Me. *Me.* ME. Their education is about how it will benefit *them* and their future. And while that's better than having no direction, it surely can't be the end of the conversation.

As I read and understand the Bible, this life (by God's design and desire) seems to be a lot more focused on *how* we can come alongside others and help *them*, more so than about helping ourselves. How we can help to make this world a better place. How we can better work with God to help see *His* kingdom come *here on earth, as it is in heaven.*

> No one can serve two masters. Either you will hate the one and love the other, or you will be devoted to the one and despise the other. You cannot serve both God and money.
>
> — Jesus, Matthew 6:24

Preparing to Fulfill God's Call

The second semester of my freshman year was much better than the first. I was a little (OK, a lot) more intentional with my studies, and I did quite well in my Organic Chemistry 1 class. I thought I had found my niche, yet I still struggled to imagine what I might do with this kind of degree. As it turned out, I didn't have to sit with that dilemma for long.

As that spring term was winding down, the time came to register for classes for the following fall term. And so I sat down at the desk in my dorm room and pulled out the academic map that my advisor (who was also my organic chemistry professor) and I had created for my final three years of schooling. As I looked at the classes, I started to thumb my way through the class catalog (sounds like an archaic process by today's technological standards) in order to get the specific class identification numbers. I began to complete my registration form (by hand, pencil and paper—today's student does not recognize such a process). I sat, prepared and confident about how I would craft the fall semester of my sophomore year.

Then, all of the sudden, it was as if God was physically present in my dorm room.

And I cannot tell you whether it was an audible voice, a Divine nudge, or some other form of holy communication, but I suddenly found myself compelled to flip past the science section in the catalog and on to the religion and ministry section.

What?

Wait . . . what?

I had *never*, in my short three years of following Jesus, *ever* considered working in a church or in any formal ministry context. In fact, I fully resisted the urge because all I could envision was the Lutheran pastors from my growing-up years—dressed in their white robes with colorful chords—and for the life of me could not see myself fulfilling such a role. (It's amazing how narrowly focused young minds can be when it comes to associating a major with a job.)

But there I was, sitting in my college dorm room, sensing a call into ministry. And I can't say that I've had many experiences where God has felt so present, and my path so clear, as I did that day.

I was both euphoric and terrified. Euphoric about such a powerful brush with God and feeling that I had been deemed "worthy" to serve God and others in such a unique capacity. Terrified at the thought of having to tell my money-minded father that my new career path would alter our plans for how I was going to pay for my side of my college debt—not to mention that this new career path involved what I believed to be a *Divine* call into full-time ministry.

As you might imagine, the conversation with my parents was a challenging one.

My dad wondered whether I could do the "ministry thing" on the side while still earning a decent wage as a chemist. I assured him that I didn't think it was supposed to work like that. Truth be told, I had neither the language, nor theological understanding, to more fully explain this Divine mystery. And so I can only believe that somehow God worked in my dad, in similar fashion to how He had worked within me because my dad did not put up much of a fight.

Sure, there were more conversations, but, for the most part, my mom and dad seemed to pretty much be onboard. My dad did regularly remind me that "ministers don't make very much money," while in the same breath also reminding me that the sizeable loans we were taking out for my education would come due six months after my graduation. His point was clear: I needed to have a plan for how I was going to pay them off.

I assured my dad that I did (or that I would) have a plan, but the truth was that I was trying my best to follow the apparent *leading* of God in my life. I was trying to be *faithful*. I wanted to be *obedient*. I didn't know where it would lead, or how I would eventually pay for it, and I didn't have to. Because, I believed, if God was truly *calling* me into ministry, then He was going to help me deal with my debt.

Now I just had to figure out how to get my organic chemistry professor/academic advisor to sign-off on my newly revised plans for the following semester.

> > >

Following God with your life, which includes your career, is a big deal. This is one of the major stumbling blocks for Christians in America. We want God, but we want the American Dream too. And if we're forced to choose between the two, well, just don't make us choose! But that's what we're suggesting to our students.

Our students have been conditioned by an American culture that is all about me and mine, bigger and better, more and more and more and more. And they've come to see how college can be a means to that end, unless, of course, Jesus gets in the way and messes it all up. His call to serve God, and not money, is one that brings us all into tension with our own version of the American Dream.

Helping students to realize the folly of this line of thinking, and exploring what a life fully availed and available to God might include, is an important and necessary element to this conversation on college. These are the years when students are being prepared and equipped for the work that they will do after they leave campus. Sure, they may go on to further education, but it's the trajectory of their lives—shaped by their education—that will launch them out into the working world. If we've been able to help them understanding their calling—regardless of the field—then it can help them to better utilize their formative time on campus.

> *True education is always about learning to connect knowing with doing, belief with behavior; and yet that connection is incredibly difficult to make for students in the modern university.*
>
> — Steven Garber, *Fabric of Faithfulness*[5]

And yes, it's worth stating or clarifying that God's call extends to *all fields* in the work world, not only the traditional mission field that too often gets associated with God's calling. God has designed everyone with different talents and passions, and a part of our work as Mentors is to help our students discover these things, as well as how God might want to use them in their future work. Not everyone will experience God's revelation on registration day. Calling is often unearthed over the course of time, experiences, and intentional conversations. And this is one of the reasons that the college experience is so important!

Think about the levels of intentionality and seriousness that our students—who feel some sort of Divine calling toward a specific field of work—will take in their studies when they begin to see how it fits in with God's big plan for their lives. How they will approach their projects and paper topics. How they will engage their field education and internship opportunities. When they're working toward a known end, a called location, the game changes. There is now good reason to take full advantage of the academic preparations they are engaged in. The correct major matters. The best opportunities matter. In a lot of ways, college becomes an issue of stewardship (as if it hadn't been all along).

The implications, however, go far beyond the classroom. Sure, that's where they will likely begin, but they can extend into other kinds of activities that students choose to get involved with around campus, as well as the local community. It impacts the kind of summer work they might pursue. It shapes the kinds of relationships, specifically with potential Mentors, that they might seek out.

> > >

College is meant to be a once-in-a-lifetime experience. It is pregnant with potential, and students need to make the very most of these very formative years, especially given the way(s) in which they are supposed to be prepared and equipped for good works in the world. Having someone like *you* to explore questions of purpose and meaning with is incredibly significant during this season of their lives.

THE MENTOR'S TOOLBOX

- Think back to your own college experience. What are some of the things you remember thinking and feeling as you prepared to head off to college?
- How many times did you change your major? How many times did you change schools? Was there a point at which you knew what you wanted to do when you "grew up"?
- What are some ways you made good use of your college years? What are some ways you wished you would have better utilized your own time on campus as a student?
- Was there someone, or something you experienced, who helped to open you up to God and how He might want to use your college years?
- How do you currently understand your own sense of "calling"? What do you need to share with your student(s) in this regard?

Take some time to reflect on these questions in the space provided on the following page.

Here are several questions that might help to promote conversation with your student in this area:

- Why are you here? Why did you choose this school? What do you want to do while you're here?
- What are your passions? Talents? Gifts? How are you currently using them? Growing them?
- What hopes do you have for your life? Where do you hope to be when you're getting ready to graduate? How about five years after you graduate? Ten years? Twenty years?
- Do you think God wants to use your college years somehow? If so, how?
- If you could do anything in the world—and money wasn't an issue—what would you do? Why?
- Do you think God can use you to make a difference in the world? If so, how do you think He might want to do this?

~ continued on the next page

- Are there ways God might want to use your gifts, talents, and passions to help meet needs in the world?
- How might your gifts, talents, and passions point toward a specific major—and future work?

For further reading on the subject of choosing to go to college, consider:
- *The Fabric of Faithfulness* by Steven Garber
- *Academically Adrift* by Richard Arum and Josipa Roksa

Notes, questions, reminders,
points of action, etc.

6
Money

Dependent » Semidependent » Independent

The blessing of the LORD brings wealth,
without painful toil for it.
— Proverbs 10:22

So do not worry, saying, "What shall we eat?"
or "What shall we drink?" or "What shall we wear?"
For the pagans run after all these things,
and your heavenly Father knows that you need them.
— Matthew 6:31–32

At a fairly young age my parents started to offer my brothers and me an allowance. We had the chance to earn one dollar for a week of "good choices" and tending to our assigned chores. The one dollar was the starting point. It was ours to lose. If our parents had to ask us to do something (like brush our teeth or put our shoes in the closet or pick up our room or a mess) multiple times, we could receive a check mark under our name on the 3 x 5 index card that magnetically clung to the refrigerator door. A check mark represented ten cents. They were trying to teach us about listening well, following directions, and being responsible. Through creating space in our home for my brothers and me to be contributors (instead of only consumers), and offering us a fair wage (so that we could begin to learn about money), we began to grow in our understanding of the intricate connections between responsibility and reward. And truly, back at that tender elementary age, there seemed to be little worse than receiving check marks and knowing that, at week's end, I would be getting a handful of change, instead of a crisp one-dollar bill.

As I grew so did the opportunities for work and reward around the house. Mowing, sweeping out the garage, vacuuming, and even dusting became opportunities to earn extra money, on top of a modest allowance, which continued to be subject to check marks.

I was probably twelve before I got my first job for which I was reimbursed by someone other than my parents or grandparents. The job was being a caddie at a local, private golf club. It was grueling work because, as you might imagine, members at private golf clubs have big bags, filled with a full set of clubs plus a handful of trick clubs—you know, just in case. As a scrawny sixth grader I did my very best to keep up with the golfer I had been assigned. And by the end of eighteen holes, my shoulders were screaming, and the rest of my body was just plain tired. But my four-plus hours of laboring in the sun had earned me a grand total of fifteen dollars, which I promptly shoved into my hooded sweatshirt as I hopped onto my bike to head for home (can you see where this is going?). My sense of pride in my work, and well-earned wage, grew as I peddled closer to home. Upon my arrival I burst through the door and pulled out . . . a five-dollar bill.

I checked my pocket again. There was nothing else to be found.

I felt sick to my stomach.

As quickly as I had burst into the house, I shot back out the door, hoping my ten-dollar bill had simply slipped out of my pocket as I parked my bike in the garage. I searched and searched some more, eventually hopping back on my bike and retracing my route all the way back to the golf course, with nothing to show for it. I peddled slowly back home, with tears in my eyes, and now all the more aware of my aching shoulders and tired body.

I learned a hard but valuable lesson that day.

And I've learned plenty more since then.

One of the most significant thoughts at that young age was probably this: It was good that I wasn't solely dependent upon myself for my survival. I was thankful, when I showed up at home with one-third of my earned wage for the day, that I still had a big meal for dinner. I was learning about earning (and handling) money while still being fully supported by my parents, who were excited to see me learn and grow in this area and knew there'd be a learning curve to my growth.

And learn I did, even up to this very moment, but some significant transitions helped to prompt much of my change.

College was a time of major transition in this area for me, and I can see how God wants to use this formative time, in similar fashion, to bring about transitions in the lives of today's students.

The reality is that the *majority* of college students arrive on campus with their financial umbilical chord still fully attached to Mom and/or Dad. There is a very real dependence upon whoever has helped to send them off to college to continue to support their students(s), who now live at a distance. Financial independence will come someday but not today (if most students have their way). And it won't come during the college years, either, because many students have certain expectations about what the college experience is supposed to be like, and about what life in general is supposed to include. And all of that requires a good bit of money, which, for now, comes primarily from their financially established parents.

While this might not sound like the worst thing in the world, far too many students are choosing to stay fully connected in this manner throughout their entire college experience. And far too many parents are enabling this kind of irresponsible behavior in their children, which is serving to reinforce some immature ways of thinking and being in the world.

Lessons of stewardship can, and really should, be learned during the formative college years, and these lessons don't only relate to fiscal responsibility but to all forms of "currency" held by our students. *Time* may be one of the biggest, most overlooked, forms of currency that our students hold. Unlike money, we are all given the same allotment of time. Learning how to manage it well is a major task. Likewise, with the rise of the Internet, and all of the technological advances that make accessing a growing body of content easily and instantly accessible—in the palm of their hands—*mental space* has become a new form of currency for this generation of students. *Money*, in this chapter, will serve as a representative of these collective forms of currency, and the need for our students to learn how to be good stewards of what they've been given—now and in the future.

The college experience is well situated to help facilitate a transition from financial dependence to semidependence (where the student is only partially dependent on their parents) to independence. And there is so much to be learned and experienced in going through this process: how to create, manage and live within a budget, how to make tough financial decisions; gaining a better understanding for how life in the real world works; as well as learning what it means to be a steward of the gifts that God provides. But when parents and students subvert this process by allowing the student to maintain full financial dependence, some long after graduation, then ramifications will be felt far beyond the *financial* future of our students.

Dependent

As a freshman in college, I maintained a job working no more than ten or twelve hours a week at a local pool. The purpose of this job was twofold: first, to maintain a nice raise and promotion that I had received over the summer, and two, to afford a couple of the minor expenses I was expected to pay for—namely, gas for my car and any spending money I wanted for going out with friends—during my first year of college. My parents paid a sizeable portion of my tuition, room, and board during my first couple of years on campus. They also paid for my car insurance, as long as I remained accident free. I didn't want for much because my parents still cared for the vast majority of my needs.

But my job kept me honest. Because I worked, I knew I had to be good about my time management (a lesson made more painfully clear after my first semester General Biology 1 grade that I referenced in the previous chapter). I knew *when* I got paid, *how much* I got paid, and *how* I would need to pace my social life if I was going to make ends meet.

And there were plenty of kids just like me on campus, and there still are today. But there were also kids who did not have to work—which is also true today. In a lot of ways I envied those kids. Their parents were affording them the full college experience (I thought). They didn't have to worry about getting up early for work or managing their schedule so they could be available for the big social events or important study sessions. Their schedule was their own, and many seemed to have an endless supply of cash to bankroll their social life. I envied them back then, but I don't anymore. In fact, I'm thankful that I had to work because I've seen how challenging the transition can be to become financially independent, especially the longer this process is delayed.

> > >

The college years are a natural time for students to begin to take on increasing levels of financial responsibility. In fact, if I could mandate a new college prerequisite, I think I would make all college students spend one year working, full time, *before* they could attend college. I believe a level of growth and maturation takes place when young people get a feel for life in the *working* world that radically changes their outlook, approach, and engagement in the college experience once they arrived on campus. When the veil is lifted, and they can see all of the time, energy, and hard work that go into a forty-plus-hour work week in order to earn that big paycheck, I think college has the potential to take on more meaning and significance.

Teaching your children to be financially independent is no easy feat. A lot of baby boomers have had to learn this the hard way. More than half of boomers say they have allowed their adult children to move back home, rent-free, according to a recent survey by Ameriprise Financial. What's more, the vast majority (93 percent) say they have provided some form of support to their adult children, like helping them pay for college tuition or a car.

— Daniel Bortz, *How to Wean Your Children Off Your Expense Account*[1]

I don't believe students would have to be at it for long before they'd start to think about more meaningful work, and how a college education could truly benefit them. The kind of responsibility and accountability they'd be exposed to in the workplace would translate into a much higher percentage of students coming to campus with direction, motivation, and a desire to more fully invest in their college educations.

But the last chapter was on college; isn't this one supposed to be about money?

Yes, it is.

But the two are intricately linked. We need to realize this, and we need to help students to realize this.

When college students are afforded an easy college life—and by easy I mean fully-funded, all-expenses-paid, nothing-withheld kind of easy—it feeds a mind-set that life can only go up from there. College students naturally believe that the kind of lifestyle they have experienced growing up in their parents' home is the kind of lifestyle that will serve as a *baseline* for them upon their graduation. College is a chance to debunk that myth, allowing students to take increased ownership of their financial responsibilities and encouraging them to find ways to make do and get by.

Now, I'm not talking about having students choose between heat and food one month, or limiting themselves to a diet of ramen noodles and Kool-Aid, for the sake of making ends meet. Many options fall on the spectrum between this (or even more extreme examples of going without) and the other end where students are afforded everything they desire.

As Mentors, we have some opportunities here. *Some* parents will have begun this journey with their students, but others might not be there yet. And money, being the sensitive topic that it is in our culture, is definitely one to approach with a great amount of caution. But we cannot afford to neglect this important topic. We need to engage our students in this area. We need to encourage them to evaluate their current level of financial dependence, and consider what steps they might need to start making toward a more independent future.

If you're serving as a Mentor to a student who is not your own child, know that parental rumblings may be directed at you, for challenging some of the familial financial constructs that are presently in place. There may be conversations with distressed, or even irate, parents because of changes taking place in their children. Yes, all parents likely desire their children to become financially independent, at some point. But some parents have predetermined *when*, and *how*, and *why* this will all happen. Some parents like to be in control here. So of all of the conversations we have with students, this line of conversation might be one of the most important for us to encourage our students to have with their parents as well.

Semidependent

I opted to move back home for my junior year of college. It was not an easy decision to make, but knowing that I was taking out considerable loans and given the fact that one of my two brothers was starting college that year (with the other brother to follow the next year), I thought it might be wise to save myself a little bit of money by taking food and housing off the table, at least for the year.

I moved back into my old room, enjoyed the laundry facility across the hall, and loved having a fully stocked refrigerator at my access. Of course, all of this was considered a perk for making a financially responsible decision. My parents understood that I was going to take on some extra hours at work, while choosing to live at home, in order to put chunks of money toward my growing college debt. I was working, volunteering at a church, serving as a student leader in the campus ministry department on campus, and attending my classes.

The big change was that I was no longer living with friends, on campus, where there were 101 different ways to be distracted by (I mean, plugged into) activity upon activity. Did my social life take a hit? Most definitely. But I had two years of established relationships that I now needed to become more intentional about, which was easier said then done. My social life became a sacrifice that moving home (and making the financially wise decision) brought about. It was a tough year socially speaking, but I got to spend a lot more intentional time with my family while investing in my future.

My intentional move toward financial independence was causing me pain in some areas of life and unforeseen blessing in others. It was a year of growing and maturing in a lot of ways—and primarily motivated by a desire to take more financial responsibility for my (present and future) life. I was making some progress, but by no means was I close to a finished product.

> *During college, continue to have open (and calm) discussions about money and the way it's spent. Earning spending money during school breaks and summers may encourage students to be more cautious with their spending habits. The ultimate financial goal is reaching graduation with as little debt as possible.*
>
> *— Parent Tips: Teaching Your College Student Financial Responsibility*[2]

> > >

A part of our work as Mentors is helping our students to see areas of their lives where God might want to work and bring about change. And in an American culture that is so obsessed with stuff, comfort, and status, encouraging our students to make painful decisions that actually *limit* their ability to have something (anything, really) is a major task. Let's be honest; we're not known for moving further away from comfort of any kind. So to think that our students will naturally (or willingly) move in that direction just doesn't make sense.

But what has been lost on many in this current generation of young people is the notion that they don't get to start with it all. The idea of starting with nothing is less than appealing to many of our students. They've been afforded much by the world's standards, and college is (supposed to be) a step toward even more. And if students aren't challenged to reconsider this line of thinking, then the stage is set for a *prolonged* financial attachment, which will adversely affect the kind of growth and formation they are *supposed* to experience during their formative college years.

As Mentors, the difficult part is getting students started. Asking timely and pointed questions and challenging students (in small ways, very small ways at first) to take on some financial responsibilities in their life can be a great start. The key is to figure out *where* God is already at work in this area because although many students will give off the air of full financial dependence, there is likely one area (if not a few) where they have actually begun to do this. Helping them to identify that area, and explore it with you, can serve as a catalyst for growth and maturation

Some of the more common expenditures college students might be expected to pay for:

1. Cell phone plan
2. Gas
3. Eating out (outside of their meal plan)
4. Coffee
5. Music, movies, and other forms of entertainment
6. New clothes

that can, in turn, create a desire for more growth and maturation through taking increasing levels of financial responsibility in their own lives.

Sometimes, all we need to do is get the ball rolling. Once started, students will (hopefully) continue the good work.

Of course, this doesn't mean that it won't be painful for them. Sure, growth and maturation is a major bonus to entering into this process, but "going without"—at any level—is not something that our students will quickly take to. But there are a couple of fairly common collegiate activities that students could be encouraged to participate in that might help to open their hearts and minds to a different way of looking at money—and what they have and what they need.

A local outreach experience (i.e., working with at-risk youth or serving meals in a homeless shelter or helping to build or repair a home in a low-income neighborhood near campus) can have a profound impact on a student. In similar fashion, being exposed to Third World conditions, while on a global missions trip, can have the same profound effect. Exposing students to other standards of life in our (local and global) world has the potential to shake students from their current ways of thinking about money and what's important. And I'm sure God can work in other ways to move students along in this transition.

But we must be willing to do our part, be it a timely conversation or challenging word or introducing students to the kind of life-altering event through which God can help them to arrive at some different (financial) priorities. Also, we must be willing to encourage students to do their parts, while leaving room for God to do what only He can do.

Independent

During my senior year in college, I lived in a house with six of my best guy friends. After spending my junior year at home, doing the "right thing" financially but struggling to stay connected with friends, I made the conscious decision to find a decent paying job, take on fifteen to twenty hours a week, and move back in with my friends for our final year together. In chapter 4 (on college) I talked about choosing to attend a private Christian college and taking on my fair share of the debt it incurred. And my comment in that section was that *I really didn't know what I was signing myself up for.* In this instance, as I chose to move back out of my parents home, and in with my friends, I had a much better idea of what I was doing.

Yes, I could probably have done myself a favor (financially) by staying at home one more year, but this time around I decided that I would attempt to have my cake and eat it too. There would be seven of us in the house, which meant that rent would be manageable. Food and gas could easily be covered with my increased hours at work, and I would still have enough left over to be able to put some consistent funds toward my school debt. Money to put toward my social life was minimal, but because I was living with my best friends, the social scene I truly desired was now within the walls of my own home.

The sacrifice(s) were different my senior year, and they continued to teach me and prepare me for my impending gradu-ation—and what I assumed would be financial independence.

No, I don't think my parents had talked about "cutting me off." In fact, I think my dad said that he would continue to pay for my car insurance until I got a job and began to prepare for the onslaught of school loans that would come by late fall, after I graduated. So by the time I was graduating, the only true, remaining financial tie to my parents was my car insurance. I can't recall exactly when I owned that final piece of my financial puzzle, but I can't imagine that it was too far into my working career. I don't know that my parents had a plan to get me to that point of financial (almost) independence by the time I was grad-uating (if they did, it wasn't one they ever revealed to me), but

I'm thankful that we found our way to that place and for all of the lessons I learned along the way.

> > >

There's no real formula to follow when it comes to helping students move toward their financial independence (and all of the potential growth that's linked to this transition). Every student (and corresponding family) will have different ideas about this and different issues to overcome in order to more fully embrace the layers of change that are possible in becoming *increasingly* financially independent. But I believe this to be an important, and often neglected, area of conversation, growth, and ownership for our students. So as Mentors, a part of our work is to venture into this realm with our students.

Learning financial responsibility is a process and not something that happens overnight. Be patient with your student and take baby steps. Mistakes are sure to happen along the way and are great learning opportunities.

— Parent Tips: Teaching Your College Student Financial Responsibility[3]

As I've previously suggested, this has the potential to be quite a delicate area with our students. But if they've started the process, and are living somewhere in the realm of "semi-independent," then there is the good chance they will be open to more conversations, and increasingly challenging levels of financial separation from Mom and Dad. So we must discerningly proceed with our students' best interest and formation in mind.

And helping our students to have increasingly "adult" conversations with their parents about their financial present (and future) is a great step toward that financial independence. Knowing that conversations about money can often get heated (because they're linked to things like responsibility, trust, and insecurities about the future), it's important to make your students aware of this going into these important conversations. In the end, our hope is that both students and parents come together on the same page (and feel good about it), in terms of the student's plan for becoming financially independent.

THE MENTOR'S TOOLBOX

- What do you remember about your own journey from financial dependence to independence? What struggles did you face? What successes do you remember most?
- How do you understand the connection between the journey toward financial independence, and growth and maturation, in other areas of life?
- What is the most significant form of "currency" that your student needs to talk about? Is it money or time or mental space or something else?
- How do you understand *your* role (as a Mentor) in this conversation, especially if you are *not* the student's parent?
- What is your biggest reservation or concern when it comes to engaging your student(s) on this topic?

Take some time to reflect on these questions in the space provided on the following page.

Here are several questions that might help to promote conversation with your student in this area:
- In what ways are you currently dependent upon your parents? What areas of your life have you "taken ownership of" since arriving on campus?
- What do you spend money on? Where do you get your money? Do you have a job? If not, why not? Would you be opposed to getting one? Would your parents be opposed to the idea?
- How do you manage your time? How much time do you spend on your studies? How much time do you spend socializing with others? How much time do you spend/waste online every day?
- As it relates to being a steward of your "mental space," how are you filtering all of the information that comes your way? How do you deal with the overwhelming amounts of content that comes your way each and every day? Do you ever feel overwhelmed? Do you ever want to ignore it all?

~ continued on the next page

- How do you understand the concept of "stewardship" that we see described in the Bible? Do you think God cares about how you spend your time and/or money? How would your "spending habits" change if you were seeking to honor God with your different "currencies"?
- How much has money dictated your thinking about college? About life after college? About the kind of work you hope to do someday?

For further reading on the subject of money, consider:
- DaveRamsey.com
- *Managing God's Money* by Randy Alcorn
- *Money, Possessions, and Eternity* by Randy Alcorn

Notes, questions, reminders,
points of action, etc.

7
Responsibility

Entitlement » Responsible "For" »
Responsible "To"

Do not think of yourself more highly than you ought,
but rather think of yourself with sober judgment,
in accordance with the faith God
has distributed to each of you.
— Romans 12:3b

"A new command I give you:
Love one another. As I have loved you,
so you must love one another."
— John 13:34

G rowing up."

These words evoke a lot of different images and emotions, and among the many other words we associate with growing up, "responsibility" is probably atop the list. Growing up speaks to (or at least it should) taking on more responsibility in life—for one's self and, eventually, for other things and people.

During our youth, we often looked forward to the day when we were all grown up and able to do whatever we want to do. We felt oppressed and restricted as a youth, unable to make decisions for ourselves, and often felt as though our ideas and opinions didn't carry much weight in the adult world. We thought (and today, they think), *Just wait! When I'm older, and can make all the decisions, everything will be different. Life will be better!*

And here we stand, alongside our young college-aged friends who are supposed to be earnestly journeying toward this place of adulthood—and more power to control the outcomes of their own lives—but that "just wait" attitude that once caused them such angst has morphed into more of a, "uhhh . . . I think I'll just wait." A noticeable resistance exists to entering into new levels of responsibility that are intricately tied into the control they so strongly desire. They've journeyed *close enough* to adulthood (and responsibility) to realize this, and are now choosing to sit at bay and wait for the time to be right.

As already highlighted in this book, the time for students to "get this" is now. As Mentors we must explore personal responsibility, or ownership, more in-depth. We also should be aware that there are different ways of understanding responsibility because our students will likely need our help with these distinctions along the way.

Many of today's college students come to campus with a high sense of self-entitlement. They're not responsible for much of anything. They believe that, for some reason, they're owed something.

Anything.

Everything.

They have been afforded a lot, for most of their lives, and don't see the need to break from such a me-centered way of life. They have learned to be consumers, in a consumeristic culture, and it will be difficult to convince them that life is supposed to look differently. Still, this is exactly what needs to occur. They will need to be awakened to the fact that life is not all about them. You will need to challenge them to learn to see the world, and all that is in it, as God does—and to grow to understand they have a role in this world beyond simply being consumers, which is more clearly defined as students grow in their understanding of responsibility.

Know, too, that as some students are challenged to take on new levels of responsibility, their knee-jerk reaction—after getting over themselves, and beyond their need to be given everything they desire—can take them to the opposite end of the responsibility spectrum, where they suddenly feel responsible *for* everything. They might be consumed with thoughts of the AIDS epidemic in Africa, the plight in Haiti, the unrest in the Middle East, sex-trafficking, the homeless man on the street corner, the unsaved on their campus, orphans *anywhere* and terrorism *everywhere*! Yes, their newfound sense of responsibility can end up feeling more like an albatross around their neck, as they attempt to swim about in the cultural ocean of pain and suffering in our world.

Without realizing what they're doing, students replace their lack of care and concern for the world with one that resembles that of the Messiah. They move from caring solely about their own needs to feeling compelled to meet *all* of the needs in a hurting world. And while this might sound like a positive move away from a life of entitlement, it's neither healthy nor sustainable.

From this place of feeling responsible *for* everything, students will need to learn how to become responsible *to* certain things. It may sound like a nuanced distinction, but I can assure you that it will make all of the difference in the world. Our students are not capable of meeting all of the world's needs, nor are they equipped to hold up under the weight of their collective awareness. Being responsible *to* something is freeing on one hand but is also a much more difficult place to live because it requires one to engage in ongoing assessment and growing awareness—of what is happening in the world and what they are responsible *to* (as well as what they are *not*). It involves learning how to be available to God while not trying to replace Him. It also involves trusting that God can, and will, use other members of the body of Christ to meet needs in the world.

But let's start back where most of our students start—and many, sadly, fail to move beyond during their time on campus—entitlement.

Entitlement

Having worked on multiple college campuses over the course of the past fifteen years, I have seen a lot. Entitlement is not a new problem. In every generation, and likely on every campus, individuals believed themselves to be entitled to something more than the general population of students. They saw themselves as different, special, and even privileged. They thought they should be exempt from some things, and receive special consideration in some areas, and never could they see themselves as being just like everyone else around them.

What we are seeing on campus today, however, is beyond this. We are increasingly seeing students who, as kids, were told they could do no wrong. They were winners, all of them. They received trophies just for showing up. They weren't taught how to lose, or be good losers. They didn't have to navigate struggles because their parents always took care of it on their behalf. Their lives, up to this point, have been controlled and made as easy as possible, all for the sake of seeing them succeed.

Their parents have been well-intentioned, but it has served to foster an air of entitlement within a much higher percentage of students than previously noticed on campus. Here are a few examples of how this entitlement has reared its head on campuses around the country:

- One colleague shares the story of how a student in class, upset about the C she had earned on the first exam of the term, proceeded to call her mom on her cell phone—while class was still in session. Sitting in the back of the class, and getting increasingly worked up as she pleaded her case to her mother, the student eventually got up and started to move toward the front of the room. The stunned professor, assuming the student was *finally* going to take her temper-tantrum phone conversation out into the hall, turned toward a different section of her class—only to then feel a tap on her shoulder. She turned to find the teary-eyed student standing at her side, holding out her phone and stating that her mom would like to talk to her.

True story.

Here's another one:

- A concerned student, regarding a book he was assigned to read in his religion class, decided to call home to talk it through with his parents. Rather than taking the counsel of his parents and approaching his professor with his concern himself, he opted to let his dad handle it. His dad decided to place a call to the school. Skipping *over* the professor, *over* the dean of the School of Religion, and even *over* the provost, the dad called the president of the university—about a book.

Here's a story that comes out of *Residence Life*.

- The daughter of a former professional athlete was moving on to campus one year. She was slated to live in a dorm room with two other first-year female students. Without contacting either one of them ahead of time, she showed up on move-in day with a truck (no, not a U-haul trailer; I'm talking about a full-size truck, capable of fitting three to five rooms worth of furniture in it), and proceeded to *fully* decorate the room, leaving only her roommates' beds untouched.

Here's another:

- On a fairly well-to-do campus in the Southwest, the staff and faculty vehicles are easily distinguishable from those of the students'—not because of where they're parked but because they are not brand new (and by brand new I mean that they could be found on campus months before showing up in a TV commercial announcing the "all new . . .").

Not to beat a dead horse, but maybe one more:

- On a campus that includes a mandatory convocation program as a part of the graduation requirements for *all* of its students, it was common for the office that oversaw this program to have a line (stretching out the door and across campus) at the end of each semester. Students were able to see their own account for the program online, and track their progress toward meeting their requirements along the way (up-to-date within twenty-four hours of a program's conclusion), but they showed up on the last day of the term to proclaim that a mistake had been made on their account (on the part of the administrator) and demanded that *they* do something to fix it!

Stories like these, unfortunately, are not uncommon on campuses across the country. My guess is, if you've worked with college students for any length of time, you've experienced this to some extent already. Entitlement continues to be a major issue that we, as Mentors, must address.

> *What is entitlement? It is the unreasonable expectation that one should receive special treatment or automatic compliance with his or her expectations.*
>
> — Karyl McBride, Ph.D., *Narcissism and Entitlement*[1]

> > >

Entitlement can take on a wide variety of looks and expressions within the student population. It is rare to see a student acting so overtly entitled that you could actually call it for what it is on first sight. Instead, for most of our entitled students (and they all arrive on campus at varying levels of feeling entitled), we'll have to engage them in conversations that reveal some things about themselves before we can know for sure how entrenched in entitlement they actually are.

What do they like? What do they think about? Who do they think about?

What are their values? What are their priorities? What's served to shape those things?

What do they want to do with their lives? How do they want to change the world (because the vast majority of them want to and actually believe that they can)? What are they willing to do, or sacrifice, in order to achieve their dreams?

Yes, it will likely take a little detective work to discern just how tight a grip entitlement has on the throat of your student(s). Once you've made some initial assessments, you'll know better how to proceed. Helping students to break free from the entitle-ment stranglehold is probably the hardest part in this process of growing in an understanding of what healthy responsibility actually is. To address this issue of entitlement you have to name it, to the student's face.

And this is difficult to do.

It's even harder for them to hear.

What you're actually attempting to communicate to students, in the nicest but clearest way possible, is that they're *selfish*. They're *self-centered*. They have a difficult time thinking about anyone besides himself or herself. They have made themselves to be the center of their own universe, and they think that everything revolves around them (or at least it should). And yes, while this has probably always been true of most people, during most seasons of their lives, the ability to post pictures, status updates, and location check-ins have only upped our capacity for narcissism and a self-centered orientation to life.

> *Whether it's rude behavior, lack of intellectual rigor, or both, we are all struggling with the same frightening decline in student performance and academic standards at institutions of higher learning. A sense of entitlement now pervades the academy, excellence be damned.*
>
> — Elayne Clift, *From Students, a Misplaced Sense of Entitlement*[2]

But who wants to hear that they're self-centered, and not the center of the world? That's one of the reasons I waited to talk about it, in-depth, until the middle of this book. I didn't want to scare you off as a Mentor. Your work and your role are so important—so needed—and at different points in the process of walking with students, it's going to require having some hard conversations with them. It's going to entail holding up a mirror and reflecting to students what you see.

And we don't know how any given student will respond.

If we're honest, this is one of the things we fear most about coming alongside students in this way—that we'll say something they don't want to hear, and that will be the end of the relationship.

But we have to trust the process. We must be faithful to the role God has called us to play in the lives of students, remembering that God's Spirit has long been at work—and then we leave the students' response up to them. We can't control it, nor should we attempt to. And in many instances, the longer we're in relationship with a specific student, the harder it can be to tell them the truth. We fear that all the investments we've made in them could be lost if we cut to deep. Yet if we are following the lead of the Holy Spirit, and we're speaking from a position of genuine love and a desire to see the student be successful, then we need to trust that God will use whatever we communicate in the ways that He desires.

Personally, this is work for me. I am not the best at cutting to the chase and calling things as they are. I don't know whether it's the pastoral part of me that desires people to be happy or whether it's the nonconfrontational side of me that simply seeks to avoid conflict

Thankfully, though, I've had the privilege of working with some stellar truth-tellers over the course of my fifteen years in ministry. I've gotten to see the impact that these kinds of interactions can have in the lives of students. Yes, they include tension and tough love and awkwardness at times, but in almost every instance I've seen students come back around to these individuals. It may have been later in the day or later in the week, or even after a few months have passed, but they returned with gratitude for the loving truth that was spoken to them.

They *almost* always come back. Why? Because someone was willing to speak the truth to them, *in love* (and I can't stress this part enough), and although it wasn't what they wanted to hear in the moment, they believe the person cares about them and only wants the best for them.

These Mentors have helped me to be brave and faithfully step into some of these uncomfortable situations for the sake of students. As students begin to own up to whatever level of entitlement they're operating out of, the pathway for growth and transition becomes much clearer. And we, as Mentors, can begin to have more serious conversations about responsibility and what implicates them in the world.

Responsible "For"

In the many years I've been working in college ministry, many different students have come to me in all seriousness to talk about their desire to quit school and go save the world (my words, not theirs). It usually comes on the heels of an incredible spring break or summer of serving the poor orphans in Third World countries, providing relief after a major disaster, seeing God move in the lives of the youth at a camp, or working with underprivileged kids in urban or rural areas—and they question the legitimacy of their time and work (and growing debt) on campus.

They feel *implicated*.

They've experienced something that does not fit with the comfortable world they had grown accustomed to, and they feel the need to set things right. They cannot comprehend how staying on campus and tending to their work as students is of any worth or eternal significance. They want to drop everything and go back to where their summer took them, a place where they were clearly *needed*, and simply love God and others in that place. They want to make a difference in the world—NOW— and they don't understand how or why completing their degree makes any sense. They feel compelled to act—NOW—because the need is both pressing and present.

Students who get to this place can become laser focused on this one thing, and it can truly present a challenge to them finishing their degrees, which often sets off the alarm in their parents. And we shouldn't be surprised if either party comes to talk to you, even if there wasn't a preexisting relationship in place. Students believe that their parents couldn't possibly understand, and parents often think that their student is losing sight of the bigger picture in front of them—and both, ultimately, hope that you might serve as the voice of reason on their behalf.

For obvious reasons, this is a much better place to operate from for students, as opposed to being stuck in the clutches of entitlement. But in many ways it's like swinging from one end of the responsibility spectrum to the other. Before, when thinking only of themselves, they couldn't fathom caring enough about others to change their present course. *Now*, they struggle to consider themselves and believe that if they don't act now then much could be lost.

They've moved from feeling responsible for nothing to feeling responsible *for* everything.

> > >

The beliefs and desires of students in this state of understanding are both genuine and noble, but what most of them haven't considered is that God is still working in that place even though they've left. God was likely working in that place *long* before our students arrived on the scene and will continue to be at work regardless of when, or if, the students ever return. Students have connected with something outside of themselves in ways that make them feel both implicated and needed, and they like this.

What students need most while in this phase of understanding is for you, as a Mentor, to be a sounding board for them. They want (and even need) you to be excited about this new thing occurring in their lives. They want to hear that you see the same value and significance in it that they see (and they believe their parents might not). They want to know that you think God is involved and that you believe *they* are (at least a part of) the solution to that particular problem. They want you to be the wind that helps to further inflate their sails, believing that their dreams could (and even should) become a reality.

And you will want to be all of those things.

And you might be able to be many of those things for them.

But what students won't want, and what you'll need to be willing to be, is someone who can also ask some of the difficult questions they have yet to consider.

> *There are too many places where we find the world's deepest hunger, and many of them appeal to us as the place where we might find our deepest gladness. When we try to do too many good things, we burn out or we tune out or we leave out someone we love.*
>
> — Scot McKnight, One.Life[3]

What about the time they've put into their education? (Can you see the link between this line of questioning and chapter 5 on college?) What about the plans and commitments they've made with their parent(s) as it relates to their education? Is there a responsibility they have to themselves (and their parents) to see their degree through to its natural end?

Do they believe that God called them to be students during this season of their lives? Is it possible that by finishing their degree, they could actually serve the people and/or organization better than by going back without it? God allowed Jesus to be prepared over the course of thirty years of life before entering into three and a half years of more formal ministry. Likewise, Moses spent forty years serving as a shepherd, being trained to lead before God used him to lead the Israelites out of Egyptian captivity. King David is another great example of a person who was prepared, or trained, in formal and informal ways that helped him in his formal leadership role. The Bible is full of stories of men and women who were trained and equipped for the leadership roles that God eventually led them to.

Do our students believe God can work in that context even when they aren't there? Is it possible that they're making too much of their own role in this situation?

I know I said that the first part of this conversation on responsibility, as it relates to entitlement, is going to be the toughest part; but the reality is, as students begin to dream big about how they might make a difference in the world, they might need you to serve as the string to their kite. You might need to help keep them in touch with reality—and it's not that their dreams are unworthy, or impossible, but that the timing might not be right just yet.

Now, in the same vein, it could be that their dream is exactly what God is asking them to do right now. As counterintuitive as it might feel to affirm students in their desire to leave college *without* a degree, if that is what God desires for them—and you're able to discern with confidence this same move—then you'll need to find ways to support them in this endeavor. Help them consider the final shift in their understanding of responsibility—from responsible *for* to responsible *to*.

And, of course, it's important for students to get their parent(s) on board as well.

Responsible "To"

If you've ever sat with a students who feels responsible *for* something for very long, then you've likely found yourself feeling the overwhelming weight that the student has placed upon his or her own shoulders.

I can recall a young woman, early on in my work with college students, who came to me in tears not long into a new school year. She had spent her summer in Africa working with orphans and had completely fallen in love with them.

She was struggling being back in the States.

She was struggling to focus on her studies.

She wasn't even interested in spending time with friends—in part because, as she gushed about her summer in Africa, they weren't responding in the ways she had expected them to. They struggled to feel the experiences to the same extent that she had, and the more she tried to communicate the joy or desperation or desolation, the more she grew frustrated with their inability to grasp Africa. So she thought it better to simply be by herself, which only gave her more time to think about Africa, and her desire to return.

She had the strong desire to drop out of school and return to Africa, her summer home—her new home away from home. She was convinced it was what God wanted her to do, but she was having a difficult time convincing her mom that it was a good idea.

The student and I talked regularly about this for a few weeks. Over the course of our conversations, her insistence that she must return to Africa started to ease up enough for her to more seriously consider finishing out the semester (which eventually gave way to the spring semester then, ultimately, her full degree). She was able to, over the course of many conversations, come to see that Africa would be OK if she didn't make it back right away. Indeed, countless others over in Africa cared *just as much* about the country, and even the same group of orphans, and that she may have been overestimating her own sense of being needed.

Those were huge steps—significant breakthroughs—that don't always pile up in such orderly (and timely) fashion. But this student was beginning the next transition in her understanding of what it meant to be responsible to (and not for) what she had seen, experienced, and sensed God calling her to.

> > >

This may seem like a nuanced distinction, but I assure you it makes all the difference in the world! This final transition is meant to bring freedom and focus to our students' understanding of what it means to be responsible. When they were feeling responsible for everything, they were putting themselves at the center of the issue and believing that all of the potential outcomes were dependent upon *them* fulfilling some significant, if not central, role in the process. In a lot of ways, being responsible *for* something is all encompassing, overwhelming, and ultimately debilitating. In this understanding of responsibility, there's no clear definition to the limits of one's responsibility, only vague notions that *everything* hangs in the balance and is dependent upon *their* full engagement. It speaks to an unhealthy, although quite invested, way of being responsible.

> *The place God calls you to is the place where your deep gladness and the world's deep hunger meet.*
>
> — Frederick Buechner, *Wishful Thinking*[4]

Becoming responsible *to* something, however, is entirely different, and this is where we want our students. Still, much like a number of the other areas I have already talked about, the challenge comes in learning how to recognize and yield to the leading of the Holy Spirit so that students know the extent to which they are responsible. When they were operating from a position of entitlement, they held *no* responsibility. When they were operating from a position of feeling responsible for something (or everything), there was a sense that *everything* was riding on their shoulders. But here, in the position of learning how to be responsible to something (or someone), students will need to learn how to discern what their *specific* responsibilities are—learning to discern what it is that's within their ability to shape, and bring change to, and what is not.

Equally important is discerning how long their responsibility to this specific issue or entity is supposed to last. In some cases it may be indefinite, but in many cases, that will probably not be true. Knowing when and why to stay, as well as when and why to go, is another decision that requires our students to lean heavy into the Spirit's leading. This can be a challenging thing to learn, especially because most students prefer to have more control over the situations they place themselves in. Yielding to the leading of an invisible, untouchable, incomprehensible Supreme entity is challenging (to put it mildly).

So this becomes a part of our work.

As Mentors we must help students to move in this direction, remembering that you cannot force them to make this transition, nor any of the others for that matter. You are a companion on the journey, a guide at times, but ultimately there to assist, encourage, question, and challenge them along the way.

And if you can help your students to recognize their need to take increasing levels of healthy responsibility in their lives, then you are indeed doing a good work.

THE MENTOR'S TOOLBOX

- Did you ever struggle with entitlement? If so, what do you recall about your own journey from entitlement to responsibility? Where do you currently find yourself on the journey from feeling responsible "for" things to feeling responsible "to" some things in some specific ways?
- What's the biggest struggle you have with talking to (or confronting) students about their entitlement? Do you believe this to be "your job"?
- How is this progression in understanding responsibility helpful for talking with students? Are there elements that are still a bit confusing for you?
- How would you talk with a student who wants to quit school to go off and make a difference *now*, without being a "wet blanket" on what he or she believes to be God's leading in life?
- How would you help students to understand and discern "the leading of the Spirit" in their life? How would you assist them in becoming more sensitive to the Spirit's work in (and around) them?

Take some time to reflect on these questions in the space provided on the following page.

Here are several questions that might help to promote conversation with your student in this area:
- What do you care about? What's important to you? What puts a "fire in your belly"?
- What are you good at? What comes naturally to you? What would you say you're gifted at? Passionate about? Where do your talents lie?
- Have you ever thought about how God might want to use your gifts? Do you think your talents and passions (as given by God) might point to something He wants you to do in the world?

~ continued on the next page

- What do you know about _____ (the quiet kid who always sits alone in the cafeteria? Or the homeless guy who hangs out at the edge of campus? Or the sex-trafficking issues in our city? Or . . . fill in the blank).
- What implicates you? What are you confronted by that draws you in and demands that you do something about it? How do you know? What do you think your responsibility is to that issue?
- What do you think the difference is between being responsible "for" something and responsible "to" something?
- How do you care about the things happening in our world without becoming overwhelmed or overly burdened by them?

For further reading on the subject of learning to embrace one's life, consider:
- *Let Your Life Speak* by Parker Palmer
- *The Call* by Os Guinness

Notes, questions, reminders,
points of action, etc.

8
The Past

Defined by Their Pasts » Obsessed about
Their Futures » Allowing God to Use Their
Pasts to Shape Their Futures

*And we know that in all things God works
for the good of those who love him,
who have been called according to his purpose.*
— Romans 8:28

*Not that I have already obtained all this,
or have already arrived at my goal, but I press on to take hold
of that for which Christ Jesus took hold of me.
Brothers and sisters, I do not consider myself yet
to have taken hold of it. But one thing I do:
Forgetting what is behind and straining toward what is ahead,
I press on toward the goal to win the prize for which God
has called me heavenward in Christ Jesus.*
— Philippians 3:12–14

The past is an interesting thing.

We've all got one.

And all our pasts speak to where we've come from. The places we've been. The people we've been with. The experiences that have shaped us. They tell the story, quite literally, of how we've become the people we are today.

All of us, each and every one, can point to different things in our pasts that could simply be classified in terms of "the good," "the bad," and "the ugly." And we're all in the same boat when it comes to our pasts; there is absolutely nothing we can do to change them. Our pasts are just that—*our pasts*. It's our very own, and it represents all of our life, up to this very moment. And no matter *who* we are, or *what* power we might wield in this physical world, we can do absolutely nothing to change what we've done or where we've been.

We all have a past.

We've all done things we're quite proud of. If possible, we would love to replicate and recreate the settings and situations that helped to foster the context that allowed for those things to occur—so we could experience them again. *And* we've all done those things that we're not so proud of. Things that have hurt us. Things that have hurt others. And unfortunately, it's often those hurtful things that tend to stick with us. They act like a stain on our shirt that we can't get rid of—and we're quite certain that everyone will judge us based on this glaring defect. These "bad" and "ugly" things from our pasts tend to hang with us and haunt us.

In fact, there are ways in which we give these bad and ugly things incredible voice, power, and control in our lives. We allow them to define us in unhelpful and untrue ways. We struggle to shake these inaccurate definitions of ourselves and begin to believe the lie that says *we are what we've done*. We are "the bad" or "the ugly" from our pasts. And that's all we'll ever amount to.

It warps our minds.

It wounds our hearts.

And it begins to put limitations on our futures. *We* begin to put limitations on our futures because we have a difficult time seeing beyond our malformed identities. We struggle to dream about our futures because we're stuck in our pasts. And the same is true of our students.

But the college years represent a new season of life. A new beginning. A do-over. A redo. They provide the kind of transitional space that can allow for starting afresh. Still, many students struggle to move forward, dragging their painful pasts with them into their new communities and contexts. They flounder and fail to believe that God can, or will, do something new in them. Because they've been hurt in the past, and become entrenched in a specific failing (or series of failings), they're unable to step into some of the transitional possibilities that come with going off to college. They remain in that place, stuck.

There are ways in which we give these bad and ugly things incredible voice, power, and control in our lives. We allow them to define us, in unhelpful and untrue ways.

Other students, however, who are able to make the transition away from their past—no longer allowing it to define them—often end up running as far from that past as possible. They recreate themselves to be something that is wholly different, and totally separate, from that past. And while this can have some (initial) positive results, it ultimately fails to consider that God may want to use their pasts to inform their future.

Helping students to reach the place where they can acknowledge their pasts—owning the good, bad, *and* ugly— while acknowledging that it doesn't define them can help them begin to consider how God might want to *use* their pasts to bring shape to their futures. It may point them toward a field of work, an opportunity for service, or a way to be involved in the local (or global) community. Still, students must be willing to sit with their pasts, and with God, long enough to understand this direction.

But let's go back to where most of our students start when they arrive on campus.

Defined by Their Pasts

College and universities seem to be increasingly filled with broken people. These are young people who come to campus having experienced something in their past that is impeding on their present and threatening their future. This experience (or set of experiences) is most often negative in nature and typically serves as the primary identifying characteristic by which a student will think of him or herself. Regardless of all of the other good things that have been a part of a student's life, the power some events or experiences hold is difficult to comprehend.

Here are a few examples that represent the kinds of issues I've seen students struggling with over the past fifteen years I've been on campus:

- Numerous students have come to campus having experienced the unraveling of their parents' marriage (at some point in their growing-up years), and they have strong ideas about what is possible "relationally speaking," and what's not. They struggle to believe that marriage is a feasible option for their future, and even have a hard time with faithfulness and loyalty at the friendship level, because of what they've been through. So they struggle to have meaningful relationships, which only serves to reinforce their beliefs about the fickle nature of people and the unreliable nature of relationships as a whole.
- Numerous students come to campus having been previously engaged in destructive behavior and/or substance abuse and hope to make a clean break, get a fresh start.

But because some of those patterns and routines are so ingrained in them, it's only a matter of time before they fall into a wrong crowd and their old destructive ways. Or similarly, they've been the victims of someone else's destructive behavior (verbal, physical, or sexual abuse), and they struggle to believe that they deserve something more, something better. And so they find their way into new relationships that take on similarly destructive patterns.

- An increasing number of students who previously participated in the hookup culture now struggle to see how true love and real intimacy are even a possibility for their future. They see themselves as "damaged goods." As unworthy of pure love. And so they do what they know how to do and engage in the hookup culture around campus.

- Along similar lines, most male students (and a rapidly rising percentage of female students) are addicted to pornography. It's warping their sense of reality and making relationships with members of the opposite sex much more difficult than they should naturally be.

- We see students who have struggled with body image issues in their pasts and have fought hard to make some level of progress toward getting it under control before arriving on campus. Soon, however, many revert back to old habits, feeling overwhelmed in their new context and wanting to be able to control something.

- And to prove my point about how good things can still have negative ramifications, we are seeing an increasing number of students who come to campus having excelled academically back in high school and now feel obligated to be a certain kind of student (with a certain GPA), no matter the cost. Their hard work and academic efforts that helped to get them admittance into the school of their choice, and maybe even a scholarship, must now be replicated. They put an overwhelming amount of pressure upon themselves to succeed, even to the point of needing consistent counseling, medication, and, occasionally, hospitalization.

I could go on, but you get the point. In increasing numbers, we're seeing students come to campus who are feeling stuck in their pasts. Some of the experiences from their pasts are following them to campus and not allowing them the chance to grow and change in the ways that college is designed to naturally facilitate.

> > >

Youth are being exposed to adult-themed content, experiences, and realities at younger and younger ages, and they don't know what to do with all of the things they're seeing and experiencing. They have no filter or capacity for understanding what they're taking in.

Often left to their own devices, they begin to explore on the Internet and experiment with their friends, with no concept of what they are doing to themselves. They have no understanding of the kinds of behavior they're normalizing, the mental and physical pathways and patterns that they're establishing, or the very addictive behavior that they are unknowingly committing themselves to, for the foreseeable future.

They are sabotaging their futures long before they ever head off to college.

By the time students arrive on campus, they've likely seen and experienced things that have shaped them (and even damaged them) in profound ways. They've done things that they wish they hadn't. Things they wish they could take back. Things they'd like to forget they've ever seen, done, or done again (and again).

Walking with students through the trials and trails of the journeys that have led them to the present is an incredible gift that you, as a Mentor, can offer. Creating the kind of "safe space" that allows them to know they can share openly and honestly, without fear of judgment, is a priceless offering that opens the doors for healing, closure, and redemption to take place.

It likely won't be pretty, or without personal pain, as you walk with students through their storied history. And it will be important to be aware of your personal limitations as you may encounter pieces of a particular student's past that is beyond your level of expertise. It is increasingly likely that the things your students struggle with will be worthy of spending some time with a professional counselor. And this isn't anything against you as a Mentor but more so about your student getting all of the appropriate assistance he or she needs in order to take steps forward in their own journey. Sometimes helping students get unstuck requires more than what you have to offer, and you need to be OK with that because ultimately it's about them and not you.

Once unstuck, most students will often flee from their pasts, choosing to focus on the infinite possibilities of their futures.

Obsessed about Their Futures

I recall a student one semester who began to experience recurring abdominal pain. He was so busy that he did his best to *ignore* the pain at first. Once he could no longer ignore the pain, he did his best to *manage* it. Eventually it got to the point where he could no longer get out of bed, at which point his roommates drove him to the emergency room of a nearby hospital.

This student was so busy that he couldn't (or wouldn't) take the time to get himself checked out, and so upon landing in the hospital, the doctors ran test after test trying to figure out what was bringing this otherwise "healthy" young man to his knees. Without finding reason for his pain, and providing him with enough medication to help manage it, he was released. Within a couple of days, though, he was back in the hospital complaining of the same unbearable pain in his lower abdomen.

I ended up spending much of the next couple of weeks at his bedside in the hospital. After numerous rounds of testing, it was decided that he would need surgery to remove a portion of his intestine that had opened up and begun to leak acids and fluids into the rest of his body. The doctor believed it to be stress induced.

I learned a lot about my young friend over the course of the two weeks I visited him at the hospital. For starters, it turns out that he had a lot to be stressed out about. As a senior, he was taking a full load, working multiple jobs, and stressing about money (and being in the hospital for two weeks was not helping this any).

I also had the chance to sit with him as he had multiple phone conversations with his mom. (This was painful even for me!) The conversations that took place over the first few days were always centered on money. I listened to my young friend try to justify to his mom that everything the doctors were doing was absolutely necessary, and that he would do everything he could to "keep costs down." My young friend was always quite frustrated by the time he got off the phone yet was able to quickly level out his emotions, sharing about how challenging his mom had it as a single parent trying to help put two kids through college. (Remember, this student was working multiple jobs so he wasn't getting any free ride.)

Our conversations eventually led to his dad, who just couldn't seem to get his own life together. It was sad to hear this young student justify his father's absentee nature and his mother's obsession with the financial side of this unfolding episode.

It took a turn for the worse when I found out that his mom was choosing to stay back home, several states away, in order to work while her son went through invasive surgery. And by day 3 of his recovery (day 5 of his hospital stay), my heart nearly came up my throat when I watched him break down while on a phone conversation with his mom, when he basically begged her to come be with him. It was all that he wanted.

His mother did *eventually* come, but I could tell that the delay had taken its relational toll on my young friend. This was one more unfortunate incident added to a painful pile of incidents that had accumulated over the course of some time. And although I hated that this young man had to endure this health and family ordeal (in front of me and others who had rallied to his side), I'm thankful that he chose to allow some of us into the more personal layers of his life.

Some students are incredible when it comes to masking the wounds and struggles of their past (and even present). And yet, I believe that the majority of them are dying to get real with someone. I've been surprised by how many times, more often while working side by side on a project of some kind (because it takes time to work up the courage, and it helps to be actively engaged in something that lessens the likeliness of eye contact), a student will begin to gush the pain of his or her past.

And these students often catch me off guard not because of what they're sharing but because as long as I've known them they've given every appearance of being someone who has it all together. They seem quite focused, even driven, toward accomplishing major goals relating to their future. They seem to know exactly what they want, which makes them stand out amidst a swelling sea of "undecided" and less-than-serious students on campus. And it turns out that their laser-like focus is just as much about overcoming their past as it is anything else.

But what's driving them?

What's shaping their goals and dreams at this stage of the game?

What's motivating them to be as focused as they are?

Likely, it is the dream of a better life, a brighter future. A time of life and a way of living that is of their own choosing and making. It probably entails a great paying job that will afford them the kind of secure and comfortable lifestyle that they feel has eluded them since their past took a turn for the oppressive. They've convinced themselves that the way of getting beyond their past simply entails a great effort. If they can work hard enough, and position themselves just right, then their future will be incredible—or, at the very least, drastically different from their past.

And sadly, some of these students end up in the hospital, like my young friend. Others drop out or need a medical leave. And still others end up taking their own life, unable to deal with the stress or other demons that haunt them.

That's why this is such a big deal.

> > >

Once students are given the invitation to leave their pasts behind, those who can run in the opposite direction as fast and as far as possible. Also to the extent that they can, they distance themselves from the people and habits they associate with their old way of living and begin anew. Without any attempt at closure or learning from where they've been (or what they've been through), they forge on ahead into new frontiers.

There's no looking back.

Indeed, there's fear in looking back. They fear that the past might see where they're going and attempt to derail them in that place—no, not physically but mentally and/or emotionally.

Regardless of whether or not your student has had to go through the arduous process of working through past hang-ups and hurts that had them struggling to move forward, *all* students eventually get to a point when they become obsessed with their futures.

As it relates to their past struggles, however, this new obsession with the future is often an attempt to forge a new existence that has nothing to do with the parts of their journey that have proceeded this new phase. They see themselves as a blank canvas—clean, pure, and without blemish. The possibilities for their future are now bright and limitless.

And while this is a move in the right direction, the inability of your student(s) to acknowledge, embrace, and learn from their past is a detriment to their future. If it's unresolved emotional trauma, it can only be repressed for so long before it bubbles back to the surface. If it's destructive behavioral patterns, one can only try hard to bring about change for so long before some of those old ingrained ways raise their ugly heads. If it's harmful ways of viewing self or others, or engaging with self or others, students won't be able to run from the unresolved issues of their pasts for very long.

Ultimately, they can learn lessons from their pasts—the good, the bad, and the ugly. And helping students to appropriately deal with their pasts can offer two things: closure and direction.

Allowing God to Use Their Pasts to Shape Their Futures

I love stories about underdogs. Unlikely heroes. People overcoming incredible odds to really make something of themselves. It reveals that, truly, anything is possible. It speaks to a God who is constantly making all things new.

Unfortunately, we don't often get to see this take place. Not because it's not occurring but because, at the college level, we're often near the beginning of the process. We get to see some of the earliest stages of the new picture being painted. We get to hear the first few lines of the new song being sung. But then our students graduate and move on. We'll have the blessing of staying connected to and even continuing to journey with some students. Others we'll lose touch with, and hopefully have the chance to reconnect with in the future.

But others, still, will come into our lives, having started this process elsewhere, and give us the chance to watch this process in some of the later stages than we're typically able to experience with many of our students. These folks are our friends, colleagues, co-workers, employees, and community. And while we weren't with them when they started on their journeys of working through their pasts, we get the chance to hear (and celebrate) the stories they share with us. No, these aren't the students we've started this process with, but based on some of their inspirational stories of change and transformation, we're able to gain some insights into the kind of work that God continues to do in our former students.

>> *The past is our definition. . . . We will escape it only by adding something better to it.*

— Wendell Berry
Standing by Words[1]

We get to see the power of God to transform a life. To heal the wounded. To redeem the wrecked. To bring beauty from ashes. And it hopefully gives us the kind of encouragement and insight that can help to bring shape to the conversations we have with students much earlier in the process. We get the chance to reap the benefits and experience the blessings of a work someone else helped to get started, and likewise people all over the world will get to celebrate the lives of those you've had the chance to start a process of healing and recovery with.

> > >

In the previous section I mentioned closure and direction, two potential (probable) benefits of standing before God with a willingness to explore all of the pains and hurts of their pasts.

Closure.

Resolution.

Redemption.

I don't believe God wants the pains and hurts of our pasts to remain open, seeping, infected wounds. Our God is a God of healing. He likes to make things new. He likes to bring peace to chaos, love to pain, and joy to the hurting. When we're willing to bring our past before God, He can do things with it that we likely never imagined possible.

It can be difficult to convince young people of the benefits of engaging in this part of their journey. It brings up so much pain and sadness that most simply prefer to leave their past where it is. Still, for closure, resolution, and redemption to take place, students will have to be willing to face their past and begin to deal with it. And as they begin to experience the peace that comes in closure, and connect the dots of their past to their present, it's possible to project a trajectory for what their future might hold.

It's one of those things that our students have likely never considered, how God might want to use their pasts to provide direction and context for their futures. It's a hard thing for most of them to conceive of during their college years, in part, because they're just beginning to deal with those deep wounds for the first time. The move away to school has provided the kind of distance necessary for students to begin to acknowledge the pain of their pasts for what it really is, which is why they're so often quick to run as far away from it as possible.

But if we can offer them a safe, judgment-free space in which to explore their "old" pains and hurts, they might begin to see how God could use their past experiences (as painful as they may be) to offer insight into their future work.

NOTE: It will be important for you, as a Mentor, to be mindful of what you are equipped to handle in this area. Recognize your own limitations, and, if needed, be willing to direct your student to the counseling services on/off campus.

THE MENTOR'S TOOLBOX

- What are the issues this chapter has raised for you in your own life? How have you gone through this process of dealing with your past? Are there unresolved issues that you need to give time and attention to?
- Do you ever remember feeling "stuck"? If so, what did it feel like? Do you remember how you got unstuck?
- Do you remember ever trying to conceal certain parts of your past from others? If so, what was behind that? What were you attempting to hide? Why? Was your "secret" ever revealed? If so, how did that leave you feeling?
- Does your current work tie into any past hurts or pains from your personal history? If so, how did that come about? How did that unfold in your life?
- What are the stories from your own life that your student(s) might need to hear (as they relate to "the past")?

Take some time to reflect on these questions in the space provided on the following page.

Here are several questions that might help to promote conversation with your student in this area:
- Tell me about your past. What are you leaving out? What inspires you? What weighs you down?
- How much have you "changed" since you arrived on campus? *How* have you changed? *Why* have you changed? Would those who were closest to you back home wonder what happened to you?
- Describe some of the events and people from your past that have served to shape you. What made those things so significant? Are there things that you didn't share? Things you might think you'd rather me not know?
- Are there issues or struggles from your past that have followed you here to campus? Are there things you had hoped would have stayed back home, that you now have to deal with, here on campus?

~ continued on the next page

- Are there unresolved issues from your past that you want to deal with during your college years? If so, what are they? How do you think we should address them? If not, why not?
- As you think about your past, your struggles or issues in particular, do you think there's anything God might want to do with those things in your future? Do those things possibly point to some sort of future work?

For further reading on the subject of dealing with one's past, consider:
- *Life's Healing Choices* by John Baker
- *To Be Told* by Dan B. Allender

Notes, questions, reminders,
points of action, etc.

9
Community

"Back Home" » Campus » Global

Two are better than one,
because they have a good return for their labor:
If either of them falls down,
one can help the other up.
But pity anyone who falls
and has no one to help them up.
— Ecclesiastes 4:9–10 NIV

My command is this: Love each other as I have loved you.
Greater love has no one than this: to lay down one's life for one's
friends. You are my friends if you do what I command. I no longer
call you servants, because a servant does not know his master's
business. Instead, I have called you friends, for everything that
I learned from my Father I have made known to you.
— John 15:12–15 NIV

On the campus I serve we host several two-day sessions of summer orientation. It takes place in mid-June each summer and is designed to get our new students onto campus for a quick visit so that we can continue the process of familiarizing them with their new campus community. We then send them back home for a couple of months before they return for good.

And only in the past couple of years I've noticed an interesting shift.

It used to be that when students showed up for this event they were meeting one another for the first time. Most students, when not with their parents, simply flew solo—or potentially took the brave step of introducing themselves to someone during one of the early sessions on day 1, providing themselves a "buddy" for the rest of their time on campus.

But with the prevalence of different social media outlets, Facebook in particular, students are taking advantage of the opportunity to "connect" long before they come to campus. Upon admittance, students are invited to join the "Class of _____" *closed* Facebook group. There, they are given the ability to connect with all of their incoming peers in ways that allow them to be as revealing or unengaged as they desire. So now, when showing up for summer orientation, students are getting to meet in person the people they've been connecting with online for weeks, if not months.

In a lot of ways, new technologies like this are serving as "game changers" in our culture. And the "Class of _____" Facebook groups are a glowing example of what I'm talking about. Students are getting the chance to jump-start the relationship-building process—safely, from behind their screens, back in the comforts of their homes—long before they ever arrive on campus.

While there are a lot of positives to this, there are some unforeseen challenges as well.

> > >

Technologies aside, community is—and always has been—incredibly important. Finding a place (or places) to belong, where one can know and be known by others, speaks to how we've been wired. We've been created as relational beings. We are hardwired for relationships. We thrive in community, not isolation. And this relational design reflects the Triune God, whom we've all been created in the image of. So it should be of no surprise that community is such a significant factor when it comes to the college experience.

But community has become an increasingly challenging thing to find in our world. With all of the advances in technology, studies show that we are more "globally connected" and yet lonelier and lacking deep meaningful relationships. Many of today's young people may be friends with hundreds, or even thousands, of people online, but find themselves with few people in their offline life to socialize with. They may feel comfortable with taking to the Web to share the good, bad, and ugly from their day, yet feel as if they have no one to actually sit down with for a heartfelt conversation.

The college years provide an opportunity to engage in quite a unique communal context. No matter how life before college was for your students, the transition to campus life provides a time and space for engaging and exploring new communities while also providing the capacity for staying virtually connected with old communities.

Leaving home, in whatever form, has always been a challenge. Going off to college has long represented the first real "step *away*" from home for young people. And while it may not be a struggle for all students, leaving home and going off to campus certainly is for many. The actual physical/geographical relocation used to help facilitate many of the other transitions outlined in this book. Leaving home once *demanded* that students take on new responsibilities in their lives that helped to further the "growing up" process. But with all of the advancements in technology, it has become increasingly easy to stay *too* connected to communities back home, which can keep students from fully engaging (or even remotely engaging) in the community life on campus. Ultimately, this has negative ramifications in areas other than communal relations.

Home is familiar.

Home is easy.

Home doesn't require any risks.

And although many students make the conscious decision to "leave home," and move away for their college experience, it's not until they're on campus (and Mom and/or Dad have left to go back home) that the reality of this choice sets in. Students can quickly become paralyzed by all of the unfamiliar and unknown. And it's become all too easy to hop online and instantly be connected with that which is familiar, no matter how distant.

As Mentors today, we need to challenge students to better engage in their new communities on campus, "investing in" the new realities of their geographical transition, to get the most from these college years. As they grow into healthy relationships in their new campus context, they can then better engage in new (and old) global relationships in better ways, including the ones back home.

"Back Home"

I'm always surprised to learn about students who go home most weekends—and really, any chance they get. In part, that's because I rarely went home as a college student, and I went to college a mere four miles from the home I grew up in. In fact, I actually had to be convinced (ahem, guilted may be a more accurate sentiment) to stop by the house every so often. I loved living in community with good friends and new friends, and probably feared missing out on anything happening on campus. I loved all of the friends I was making, all of the fun things we were doing, and didn't want to interrupt my social life in order to make even a quick stop back home.

Now I'll admit, I probably benefited from the fact that I went to college with two of my very good friends, and I continued to live in the Twin Cities area where I had spent all of my life up to that point—little was unfamiliar to me. If that had been different, I may have been more inclined to go home when the opportunities presented themselves.

Maybe.

But I don't think so.

I knew my family was there if and when I needed them, and I was loving campus life! Sure, I made it home for special events— birthday, holidays, special family gatherings. For the most part, however, I lived as if I was hundreds of miles away from home (much to my mother's chagrin). And yet, I'm sure that having many of the comforts of home made being away from home that much easier. Great friends, familiar area, and the knowledge that I could leave campus and be in my parents' driveway in seven minutes had more of an impact on me than I'm sure I realized at the time.

I had peers, however, who didn't feel the same way I did. They went home more often than I did. Much more often.

> > >

For many students, moving away from home is the first *big* disruption to the life they've always known. For many others, this is one among a series of disruptions, which further serve to foster feelings of instability and uncertainty in their lives. Either way, most students feel a pretty significant "shock" to their system when they move away from home to attend school. And of all the changes that take place as a student transitions into college, the most difficult is likely the change in community.

Students have spent the better part of eighteen years cultivating relationships, and relational contexts, that they now are giving up (unless they go to school fairly close to home as I did—and as so many others do). Their relationship with their parents, regardless of how great (or tumultuous) it might have been, will be a challenging one to see change. Likewise, moving away from good friends—in many cases, lifelong friends—can be equally difficult. Even if your student goes to school close to home, their friends might not, which means that those relationships will likely change at some point along the way. Other important relationships—with relatives, pastors, coaches, professors, and so on—all will be challenged to change in this season of transition.

>> *Generation iY (born between 1984 and 2002) loves using technology to communicate, but they also enjoy the isolation and control that technology gives them. . . . The trouble, of course, is that it's hard to develop real relationships in an unreal world.*

— Tim Elmore,
Generation iY[1]

And that's OK.

In fact, that's *supposed* to happen. College is supposed to be a time of transition, which naturally will bring changes to relationships. Some will continue on but undergo changes, like the relationship between parents and their young adult children. Friends who stay in the area will remain close, but as both sides begin to venture into new circles (different schools, work and school, even same school), changes will occur. Relationships with other significant individuals will likely change as geographical proximity grows, contact regularity decreases, and time passes.

Or at least it's supposed to. But with the rise of a number of technologies that make staying connected easy and inexpensive (if not free), more and more students are staying more closely tied to their communities back home far longer than they previously have.

Gone are the days when distance meant *distance*. When students had to call long distance if they wanted to connect with someone outside of their immediate area code. When saying "good-bye" meant "I'll see you the next time I'm home," instead of "the next time I'm online." Today's student can literally talk face-to-face (albeit through a screen) with anyone around the world (as long as they have the technology—and increasingly, they all do).

Instead of being forced out of their dorm room to connect with members of their floor or hall, students can sit on their computer and Skype or Facebook with friends and family back home. Instead of taking the time to connect with new classmates before or after class, it's much more likely that new students will opt to call or text with someone familiar, back home. When troubles arise, old relationships are most definitely the first option for support and encouragement.

While this might not seem like such a big deal, consider the possibility that by the time your student is finally ready to start making some more intentional and meaningful connections on campus, many of the social circles once open and fluid (during the early weeks and months of their academic career) are now closing, if not closed. Delaying engagement in relationships on campus can have unexpected social ramifications. This will, in turn, drive your student all the more back toward those friends and familial relationships at home.

Add to this the fact that by staying more connected back home it will become increasingly challenging for the student (and the parents) to see themselves as transitioning to a new relational state of being. So even though the student may want to *believe* themselves to be grown, or growing up, it will remain easy for them to continue to live dependent upon old relationships and relational paradigms, most specifically that of parent/child. Although they'll want to do grown-up things, it will prove to be a lot easier to let Mom and/or Dad take care of it, especially if they are willing to oblige, which they seem to be in increasing percentages. This, obviously, will serve to undercut a lot of the growth, transition, and development that I've already talked about in this book.

Most students, if left to their own devices, will eventually begin to make this transition. Some won't, however, at least not without some nudging. And others will need to be encouraged to do this a little earlier than they might naturally choose to if left to their own timing. Parents need to be willing to do their part in helping (or allowing) their child to transition in this regard, and those of us who work with college students need to be willing to do our part to invite them in to community in their new context.

I'm not suggesting an all-out abandonment of relationships back home, but in order to have healthy relationships on campus, some separation from the old, familiar relationships, may be necessary.

Campus

As I mentioned earlier in this chapter, I loved college, and I was quick to adapt to my new community. I enjoyed meeting new people and making new friends. I sought out ways to get involved in different events and subcommunities around campus. Bible studies, intramural sports, and the occasional study group eventually gave way to leadership opportunities (both on and off campus), club sports, and a growing collection of friendships and mentoring relationships.

I was quickly becoming a part of the campus community— a previously unfamiliar community to me—though it had long been nestled away between a web of roads I drove almost daily. I may have gotten glimpses of different buildings as I sped past entrances to campus, but never did I even consider an exploratory drive through the campus itself. Lack of familiarity quickly gave way to a loving obsession with my new surroundings. I simply enjoyed my new "home" so much that I had little, if any, desire to leave it. A job off campus and the chance to get to church were about the only reasons I regularly left campus.

> *College friends are somewhat different than friends from high school because you bond in different ways. You may bond during late night study sessions, making dinner together, or during long drives home. In a way, they're somewhat like your family away from home.*
>
> — www.education-portal.com[2]

All of this, of course, did not sit well with my mom. As I mentioned in chapter 4, on life lens, my mom had grown up in a fairly unstable home, which led her to create the kind of home environment every kid would be lucky to have—and likely not be eager to leave. So seeing me go off to college only a few short miles down the street had to have *initially* seemed like the best-case scenario.

Until I didn't come home.

It wasn't that I was trying to avoid my family; I simply wasn't making them a priority among all of the things I wanted to be a part of *on* campus (which sounds horrible to write—even twenty years after the fact). In my mind, I seriously could not spare a moment. I just didn't want to miss anything happening in my new community. In fact, I was so obsessed (or maybe better put, so negligent toward my family) that when I started volunteering at a church my sophomore year, literally driving past my parents' driveway two to four times a week (without as much as a pop-in), my mom had to call me out on my pathetic priorities.

My new community had so captured my attention that I wouldn't give time nor space to any other. It had to have felt like abandonment to my family—my mom in particular. But thankfully, my parents had lived enough life to recognize my infatuation for what it was, and graciously gave me the space to play it out.

> > >

If one of the biggest relational struggles college students have is disconnecting from home in order to better connect on campus, then a distant second is to actually stay connected back home. Again, this is a lot less likely to happen, especially given all of the technologies that make it both convenient and nearly effortless. And yet, it will be a struggle for some.

For one reason or another, some students will either intentionally set out for college with no desire to stay connected to their past relationships, or they will simply fail to make them a priority. In many ways it's equivalent to some of the other black-or-white situations I've talked about in this book. It's simply easier for most students to either be engaged and attentive to their relationships on campus—in their new community—or to the old ones back home. Attempting to juggle both at the same time can prove to be too challenging for some students to want to learn to navigate. And it will be especially confusing to the students who struggle to disconnect with their community back home, in order to better connect with their new community on campus, to be challenged to be better connected back home, *again*. But this will be the challenge (or for some, the tension) they need to be encouraged to live into.

The reality is, in this season of transition—the college years—students' relationships back home do need to take on a different look, feel, and level of priority. But they shouldn't be ignored. Yes, students need to find ways to branch out and invest in their new campus community—that's one of the biggest reasons they're not back home taking classes online—but it should not come at the cost of a lifetime's worth of relationships.

There's got to be a balance.

Global

I don't recall specifically what it was that prompted me to make time with my family more of a priority than it had been at the start of my college career, but I know that at some point along the way we started to connect more. At first it might have had something to do with their invitations to grab coffee or a meal—pure gold to college students after the initial charm of the cafeteria wears off. But it eventually became a special—even sacred—time, riddled with rich one-on-one conversations, which seemed to evidence a changing dynamic in our relationship. I was growing up, and (or) my parents were treating me as if it was indeed happening. A willingness to show me (and my growing independence) some respect went a long way in boosting my confidence and encouraging further growth and maturation. It also helped me begin to appreciate and respect all—*all*—the things that they had done (and were doing) on my behalf.

My parents beginning to treat me as an adult was causing me to both think and act more like one. Now, don't get me wrong; I didn't grow up overnight, and I've got a group of college friends who would quickly attest to this fact. Change, however, was definitely occurring. As it did, I think it helped to set the stage for living with my family for my junior year of college. I was a different person when I returned home because of the ways in which I was allowed to live and grow and be responsible during my first two years on campus.

This same move home, while serving my familial relationships quite well, did put a strain on my friendships back on campus. Most of my friends had moved off campus that year as well, which meant that I couldn't conveniently swing by their on-campus abode before or after class. I had to figure out how to manage my time—my life—so that I could engage in the different communities that mattered to me. On top of these two important populations, I played club volleyball (and thankfully two of my great friends were a part of that community) and took on leadership in a couple of different ministries on campus (which also provided opportunities to connect with good friends)—it all required a bit more *intentional effort* than it had before.

I'm thankful for the lessons I learned through this process because I'm not sure I could have survived otherwise after college, when God led me from Minnesota to south Florida for my first job.

> > >

Relationships are such an incredible gift from God, but man, can they be tricky. Not only do we bring our own issues into each and every relationship we enter, but we enter into relationship with people who all have their own sets of issues. And as we come together, we rub off on each other, shaping one another in both big and small ways, and this, of course, can lead to changes in most (if not all) of our other relationships.

The ways in which this happens during students' growing-up years will likely speak to how easily they will separate from their early friendships and familial relationships when they go off to college. It will likely also point to how easy (or difficult) it will be for your students to transition in their relationships and ultimately find their way to a healthy, growing relational dynamic within both old and new communities.

Community will always be a priority—indeed, a necessity—throughout life. The college years provide a good context within which students can learn how to connect, grow, and appropriately prioritize their relationships, before they embark into the great unknown that lies beyond the graduation platform.

As important as our early childhood, middle school, and high school relationships are, it's more often the relationships we make in college that become some of our lifelong relationships (regardless of geographical proximity). Likewise, the ways in which we learn to relate to adults (our parents in particular) and other friends during the formative college years will set the stage for our ability to be healthy in communities long after we leave the campus.

THE MENTOR'S TOOLBOX

- What do you remember most about your community during college (if you attended)? What made it memorable? How did it serve to shape you? What do you miss from those years on campus?
- How do you remember juggling your relationships "back home" and your new ones on campus? Do you remember this being an issue? Do you think it would be more of an issue for you today, given all of the technological advances that have been made?
- What do you see as some of the biggest relational challenges your student(s) face in leaving home? Are there common hurdles? Are there ways in which your institution addresses any of these challenges?
- What advantages and disadvantages do you see technology creating for your student(s) in this transitioning reality? What do you wish they didn't have available to them? How do you wish they would utilize these technologies differently?
- How would you encourage the student struggling to connect on campus?

Take some time to reflect on these questions in the space provided on the following page.

Here are several questions that might help to promote conversation with your student in this area:
- Where are you finding community? What does that look like for you? How important is this in your life? Why?
- What did community look like for you back in high school? How has it changed since then? How have those changes been good? Where have they been a struggle?
- Where are you plugged into community on campus? Are you connected to a local church community? Are you a part of other communities? What are they? How is each important to you?

~ continued on the next page

- How is your relationship with your parents? How has your relationship with your parents changed since you went off to college? How has it stayed the same? Are there things about these changes (or lack thereof) that are frustrating to you? Do you think your relationship is changing in all the ways that it should be? If so, how? If not, why not?
- How are you learning to be "present" and engaged in relationships in your communities here, as well as back home? How is this a challenge? How is it a blessing?

For further reading on the subject of community, consider:
- *Life Together* by Dietrich Bonhoeffer

Notes, questions, reminders,
points of action, etc.

10
Intimacy

Meeting "My" Needs » Meeting Others' Needs » Healthy Relationships

Do not arouse or awaken love
until it so desires.
— Song of Songs 8:4

Love is patient, love is kind.
It does not envy, it does not boast, it is not proud.
It does not dishonor others, it is not self-seeking,
it is not easily angered, it keeps no record of wrongs.
Love does not delight in evil but rejoices with the truth.
It always protects, always trusts, always hopes,
always perseveres. Love never fails.
— 1 Corinthians 13:4–8a

The previous chapter, on community, spoke to our design as relational beings, and our need to be engaged in life-giving relationships with others. This chapter, on intimacy, is a natural follow-up because entangled within our design as relational beings is a very real longing to be known deeply, and intimately, by another. And this most assuredly means something more than sex yet often gets confused with it, and even narrowly limited to it.

By the time students arrive on campus, they have been shaped for about eighteen years by a variety of mediums in regard to what intimacy is, how it is obtained, and why it should be pursued. Sadly, pop culture and media are the two mediums that tend to be the most influential forces of these ideas in our students, which means that their understandings of "intimacy" is often skewed in ways that are harmful and inconsistent with what God intended. What students have seen displayed on TV shows, in movies, news outlets, magazine covers, Internet sites, celebrity tweets, and so forth, rarely reflect our Creator's hopes and desires. This often leaves students confused. Yet due to such early exposure to adult-themed content, their desire for intimacy has been prematurely awakened, and so many choose to experiment with different forms of intimacy.

Sadly, this means that most of our students come to us having heard, seen, and even experienced more than they should have at their tender age—and they're wounded as a result. Many are addicted to pornography, highly skeptical of marriage, engaged in the hookup culture, and struggle to understand how (or why) to have a "real" relationship with a member of the opposite sex.

Other students will come to us struggling with commitment issues from the other end of the spectrum. They have found their way into something that seems quite meaningful and real, and in order to prove their love, they often surrender all of their personal rights—and, to some extent, even their identity. They become so committed to the relationship and the other individual that they are willing to do (just about) anything to make it work. To the exclusion of other significant relationships, and/or their own well-being, they make this other individual the center of their universe.

And while this might be a better option than the hookup culture, it can be equally harmful—in the lack of outside relationships they have (that tend to serve as a level of checks and balances) and in their ability to recognize potential abuses that are readily present in this kind of devotion, sacrifice, and self-giving.

During the college years, students' ideas about intimacy and healthy relationships may be challenged, and even changed. In similar fashion to responsibility, students' ideas about intimacy should transition from being focused on self to being focused on others, and ultimately end up in a healthier place, which considers the needs of both self and others. This transition in the area of intimacy will constitute significant work in order to overcome the loud and consistent voice of pop culture and the media.

The work and example of the Mentor will be crucial to students in this area. They need to see healthy relationships being lived out. They need to be able to see it, ask questions about it, and eventually try it out for themselves. As the Mentor, you may feel the need to have it all together relationally in order to allow students into this realm of your world, but a perfect relationship would be misleading and unhelpful to young students. Instead, what they need to see are two people who care deeply for God and each other, and are willing to do everything in their power (while allowing God to do what only God can do) to live well in the most intimate of relationships.

Let's look more closely at this journey toward intimacy.

Meeting "My" Needs

NCMO (pronounced "nick-mo") was a term I remember hearing when I was a college student. It stood for noncommittal make-out—fooling around with no strings attached. It was all about the physical, with no obligation toward commitment. And from what I could gather, it wasn't something that was widespread on my campus, nor was it a badge of honor that students wore (at least not most).

It did, however, speak to a relational paradigm that was broken—or perhaps, in the process of breaking. It spoke to a desire to experience freedom without acknowledging or accepting the corresponding responsibility. It was about personal gratification without much regard (if any) for the other person engaged in the same physical act.

NCMO wasn't (and isn't) the only way to selfishly pursue intimacy. For many others, the selfishness had more to do with "having someone" than it did having someone to make out with, at least initially. The primary "need" wasn't physical but relational, an emotional connection with another that created space to be safely "known"—or maybe it had more to do with simply not being "alone."

This was me in college. I liked the idea of having someone, of not being alone. My primary desire was to know that I had someone by my side, and I gave little consideration for the other. Before long, however, I was exposed in my selfish relational ways, as some of my friends pointed out that I seemed to liked the pursuit—or "the hunt"—of another individual much more than anything meaningful or long-lasting. In fact, my relational ways eventually led me to receive the unflattering nickname of "the three-month king," for that was the longest most of my "relationships" lasted. Once the newness had worn off, I was sadly in need of someone new to pursue.

I learned a lot the hard way during my college years of attempting to relate to the opposite sex. I'm grateful my wife didn't know me back then because I don't think I would have had a chance with her had she seen my juvenile, self-centered approach to relationships. And I'm sorry to those who were unnecessarily hurt as I recklessly approached relationships with the primary purpose of meeting my own needs.

Now, here's one final pathetic example from my own painful journey through college relationships: the break-up. So if being about "the chase" wasn't bad enough, my approach to breaking things off with my unsuspecting "significant other" was like a drone strike. From out of nowhere I dropped the bomb that things were over, and then I'd be gone, never to be heard from again. I often rationalized that it was "for the best" because I didn't want to give the other person any reason to believe that we might get back together, which stems from my own high school dating relationships (I was on the other side of this equation, always reading into my ex's charitable interactions with me). And while this might have provided some validity to my approach in college, what I ultimately communicated to the person I was breaking up with was that I didn't care enough about her (or myself, really) to do the difficult work of ending things the correct way. It's embarrassing to confess now, all these years later, but it's the truth.

And these examples are from back in the mid-1990s.

> > >

By now you've likely become familiar with the term "hookup culture" that's being used to describe the primary (yes, primary) relational paradigm of our younger generations. Typically, out of a male's desire to have certain sexual desires met and a female's desire to (hopefully) find love and true intimacy, students are hooking up. It's a term that can literally mean anything from having sexual intercourse to something as minor as hanging out with only one member of the opposite sex. Students are OK to leave this term vague and open to interpretation because it allows some to claim more and others less sexual engagement and promiscuity—without ever having to say anything at all.

>> *When the need for intimacy in a relationship is not met, we look for an "instant" solution. Where do we look? Physical, mental, social, emotional, or spiritual? It's the physical. It is easier to be physically intimate with someone than to be intimate in any of the other four areas.*

— Dick Purnell,
www.everystudent.com[1]

But the paradigm is clear in its aim. It's all about *me*.

It's about getting needs met, or perceived needs, or doing the things one thinks he or she needs to do in order to get what they want. It's about engaging in physical intimacy or intimate acts without any perceived emotional connection or association.

It's sad. It is damaging our young people at their very core. And what's worse, our young people don't even realize all of the damage that's being done. They're engaging in reckless adult behavior and being shaped in ways that will make future relationships incredibly challenging (if not impossible), to fully commit to.

And it's all for the sake of meeting needs *right now*.

Please, allow me to reiterate. It's about immediate gratification with no consideration for future (or even present) ramifications, as it relates to their ability to engage in a committed relationship with another individual. Young people are sabotaging future intimacy for fleeting, feel-good experiences. And strangely, as if totally unfamiliar with what intimacy really is, many of them equate these fleeting moments—or series of fleeting moments—to true intimacy. Why? Because it's what they've seen on display in the media. It's the influence that normalizing pornography in our culture is having on young hearts and minds. It is the influence that divorce is having on the way our students consider commitment—they've seen the underbelly, what relationships look like broken and splintered. So, they believe, it's easier, safer, to engage in something as dreadful as the hookup culture.

We have created a generation of consumers; they are products of a consumer-driven culture.

Our students have been taught, starting at quite a young age, that their needs are important and should be met. As they have grown, they have become convinced by the culture (and possibly even some of their most significant relationships) that their needs should *not* be denied. That they should seize whatever their hearts desire. That their every whim and obsession should be given in to. That they should deny themselves *nothing*.

When students leave home and head off to campus, many take these ideas and mentalities with them because they've never been taught (or modeled) anything different, which makes the unstructured environment of campus life a potential breeding ground for disaster. With more independence and less parental supervision, students are expected to navigate relational waters with self-control and sound judgment. But if their history, or the culture they step into on campus, speaks to something else, then it is highly unlikely students will find their own way into responsible intimacy. Instead, they'll settle for safe, casual hookups that will allow them to be emotionally disconnected from the physical intimacies they're engaging in with relative, if not complete, strangers.

Sound scary?

It should.

The fear of commitment exhibited is poor ground for strong relationships in the future. Instead, it reinforces what many of them have come to believe: relationships aren't worth investing in because they eventually go away. They're fleeting. They're unreliable. And, therefore, they believe they'd be wise to "get theirs" while the gettin's good.

Sure, some think—even *dream*—that someday they'll be able to get out of the game and settle down into something real and meaningful. But what they don't understand is that college is just as much the real world as is life after college. Yes, the playing field is different, but the game is still the same. And the reality is, the way(s) they learn to operate within relationships while in college are establishing (or reinforcing) a relational paradigm that will be harder to break the longer they remain in it. It's setting the stage for how they will think about and engage in relationships for their foreseeable future.

As I've established throughout the course of this book, college is a time for students to transition into (or toward) adulthood. A piece of this transition—a relatively big piece—comes in this area of relationships and intimacy. Learning that relationships are not only about having their own needs met is one of the first lessons that many of our students will learn.

Meeting Others' Needs

As a relatively new Christian when I went to college, I was eager to bring my faith to bear on my relationships, especially my dating relationships. I know this probably sounds a little difficult to believe given the sad relational dynamic I described in the previous section, but it was true. I wanted to be a servant. I wanted to set aside my own needs so that I could better tend to the needs of my significant other. Because I attended a Christian college, plenty of good Christian girls were well aware of what they were looking for in a good Christian guy—someone who would put them first, someone who would exemplify Christ.

I wanted to be this—I know I did. But the roots of selfishness and self-serving ways run deep, and the reality is, I had rarely seen this kind of relational dynamic modeled. I can look back now and see that my own mom and dad modeled this kind of self-sacrificing love for one another, but what college student thinks about modeling their own relationships after their parents? I know I didn't.

Instead, my desire to "serve" defaulted into simply being present, all the time. In fact, I'm quite certain that my college friends would tell you that I "sold them out" anytime I started dating someone new (which, as I've previously mentioned, was every few months). Whether it was insecurity or a desire to be loved, I often set aside other relationships (and other important obligations, such as sleeping and homework), in order to spend time with my new special someone. And there were other students on campus just like me. We were obsessive. Our young relationships quickly became the center of our universe, and that's not uncommon (especially on smaller campuses) during the college years.

The nature of campus life is such that relationships are often expedited because of the length and frequency of time available to commit to them. Students regularly stay up until the early hours of the morning just hanging out. And depending on the campus culture, and against better judgment, those late nights can turn into sleepovers and/or having breakfast together the following morning. Separation is possible, for a few hours of class, but there's the potential of connecting briefly in between classes (again, depending on the size of campus) maybe lunch or dinner (or both) together, or a walk around town and/or a movie before another late night of hanging out. Because students' schedules are flexible and easily manipulated, it's not uncommon to see major shifts in how (and where and with whom) students will spend their time once they're involved in a serious relationship.

Often, one or both parties in the relationship get to the point of rearranging much of life in order to be with the other person. This can even lead to, or include, taking on many of the other person's tasks or tending to his or her needs—in the name of love and sacrificial service. This could include things such as grocery shopping, cooking meals, cleaning up after them, taking care of their car, paying for different things, taking care of them when they're ill, and even doing assignments for them. Yes, some of this can be sweet and even appropriate as relationships grow and develop, but a number of relationships every year take on unhealthy levels of sacrifice and service.

And it can be all too easy for one member of a relationship, to take advantage of the well-intended desire of another, to be a giving servant. The very person who's supposed to be reciprocating the sacrifice and devotion can become the person who uses, and even abuses, the person he or she cares about. This kind of sacrificial service, mutually reciprocated, is designed to be lived out within the context of a committed, loving marriage. Students who choose to engage in this behavior do so prematurely. They're not ready for this kind of sacrifice, service, or commitment because they're still young and figuring out much of life, and their relationship will more than likely not end in marriage. Even if it does, the levels of sacrifice and service should be genuinely measured prior to marriage.

> > >

One of the big relational paradigm shifts that we hope students are able to make during their formative college years is from self to others. Practically speaking, being able to consider the feelings of others is an important step. Learning how to compromise in good and healthy ways, and not getting their own way, is a major step in the right direction!

Still, because of their black-and-white, on-or-off, all-or-nothing approach to life, it can be easy for many students to jump from a self-centered way of living to an others-centered way of living that is actually quite unhealthy. (And in some cases, like me as a college student, you can actually find instances where both extremes—selfishness and self-sacrifice—are expressed at the same time in an unhealthy relational dynamic.) And if you've been around college students in particular, then you've likely seen at least some who have found their way into relationships only to then disappear off the grid. Once active and engaged in a variety of relationships and activities, they go MIA, until they turn up (attached at the hip) with their new significant other. It seems as though they've found true love, but upon closer examination, we learn that sacrifices are being made (many times in lopsided fashion) that are not healthy at all. These sacrifices will be justified (by one or both sides of the relationship) as love, but to the seasoned observer (and when it's bad enough even the less-seasoned observer), it is quite clear that things are amiss. And getting the student alone long enough to have an exploratory conversation about such things can be nearly impossible.

When students are in this kind of relationship long enough, their priorities can change, along with their personalities, to the extent that when (or if) the relationship ends, there is not only a season of extreme mourning but a literal crisis of identity. The wounded student will have given so much of him or herself to this other individual that they can no longer see themselves without the other. It is commitment that's been pushed to an unhealthy extreme, and it's something you, as a Mentor, need to be on the lookout for.

Your students will need you to be a truth-teller, a voice of reason, even if it doesn't sound as if they're hearing you. It might feel like you're stepping on toes or sticking your nose where it doesn't belong—and even putting your relationship with this student in jeopardy—but the reality is, if their relationship gets to this unhealthy extreme, they're no longer thinking clearly. And if you sense the Spirit leading you to share the truth, in love, then you need to be faithful to that leading, and trust that God will take care of the relationship as He sees fit.

Healthy Relationships

My wife and I recently celebrated our twelve-year wedding anniversary. Given some of my relational dysfunction I described earlier, I say, "God is good!" And I'm living proof that God can use our past experiences to identify in us areas that need to be addressed, as well as shape us and mature us for future work and relationships.

We've been married for twelve years and have had a growing family for the last seven-and-a-half years. In fact, between the times I pen these words and you read them, our fifth child will have been born.

Our time together, *before* we had kids, was vitally important for our relationship. We made a lot of relational investments staring back in our early days together, knowing that this parenting season would be incredibly full—and we're reaping the benefits of many of those investments. Don't get me wrong; we're by no means perfect. But we are committed to God and to each other. And by God's grace, He continues to grow and bless our relationship and family. We experience many of the same relational challenges that most do, but we try to keep it all in perspective (with God's merciful assistance).

From time to time students, usually recently engaged, will seek us out and ask to spend some time together as they prepare for their own marriage. I think the first few times we were asked, Heather and I looked at each other and thought, *Uhh . . . I don't know that we're ready for this. Do we really know what* we're *doing? Do we really have anything to offer another couple? What if we mess them up?*

The truth was, and still is, that we are in the process of figuring out a lot of stuff for ourselves. Neither one of us came from the "perfect" home—there's no such thing—but from what we were able to glean from our own parents, as well as some of the older couples we were fortunate enough to encounter at work and church, we pieced together some ideas of what a good, healthy relationship is. And because we had benefited from our interactions with other imperfect couples—in whatever capacity they came—we eventually drew the conclusion that we would prayerfully enter these times with engaged students with hope that they would hear what could benefit them.

With each couple who we've had the opportunity to journey with, we've found that we didn't need to be perfect (in fact, the young couples were all quite relieved to know that we weren't, and that they wouldn't be expected to be so either). We were given the chance to share some of our story of learning to love God and each other well, and that proved to be exactly what was needed.

> *Being married and having children, despite their declining proportions in the United States at large, are tightly woven into the future expectations and life scripts of culturally mainstream American teens.*
>
> — Tim Clydesdale,
> *The First Year Out*[2]

> > >

Healthy relationships.

They can feel as elusive as Big Foot or the Loch Ness Monster to be sure, even though 99.9 percent of people entering into relationships likely would claim that it is what they desire more than anything. A good, healthy relationship. Someone they can be real with. Someone they can talk to. Someone they can know and be known by intimately. Someone who can see the good, bad, and ugly within them and still love them. Someone who will love them in sickness and health, richer or poorer, good times and bad. Someone they can do life with, a traveling companion for the journey of life.

No games.

No strings.

No funny business.

But lots of love, laughter, and loyalty.

And we have to imagine that this was God's desire and design from the very beginning. Adam and Eve were created for each other in ways that were life giving and *mutually* beneficial. With the fall of man, however, came the fall of relationships. We became self-centered and self-serving in our relationships, and yet must have still believed, deep down, that something better—more Divine—was available to us.

So we've gone off into the big, big world in search of it . . .

and, likely, struggled to find a good example of what a healthy relationship really looks like.

Why?

Because although we know what we want, we're still imperfect people, attempting to live in close relationship to one another. Every movement toward health and good relations is a gift from God and a move away from the ways of the world. It's a yielding to God's Spirit in our lives and in our relationships. It's nothing we can humanly manufacture or manipulate, but it does absolutely require our intentional effort. It involves the kind of self-sacrifice that I described in the previous section, while at the same time being mindful of our own needs.

In similar fashion to the chapter on responsibility, in which we explored the distinction between being responsible *for* and responsible *to* someone (or something), a healthy relationship requires that same kind of attention to detail. We learn how to be aware of, and attentive to, the needs of another while not neglecting our own needs (or allowing them to be neglected by another). It involves sacrifice but not allowing ourselves to be taken advantage of. It's mutual sacrifice and submission. It entails a willingness to give up one's power and rights while at the same time guarding against abuse of that vulnerability. As time proves good health, one's guard is eventually replaced with much higher levels of trust.

It truly is growing closer to God while growing closer to the other person.

And this is one of the reasons it is so elusive. It requires much that feels risky and out of one's control. Yet, if college students can catch a vision for this kind of relational paradigm while on campus, then they have a much better chance of adopting it for life. The college years are so formative in nature that when students have the chance to both see, and begin to practice, healthy relational attitudes and practices, it is much more likely they will continue to live out of that paradigm, even if they don't find their future spouses while in college.

As a Mentor, it's your job—a part of your task—to model this kind of healthy relationship, but this may be easier said than done. If you're married, it's not expected that you'll have a perfect relationship with your spouse, but it does need to be one that you are intentionally and prayerfully investing in, such that you can say to students, "We may not have it all figured out, but by the grace of God we're giving it our very best effort." And if you're not married, how you conduct yourself in relationships, of all kinds, will be significant. Students are watching, all the time, and they'll take notice of any place or circumstance in which your words and your life don't match up.

Much more could be said about intimacy and the pursuit of intimate relationships, but those are conversations for another time. It is important, however, that you know this will be a significant topic for your students. As your relationships grow, your students will undoubtedly come to you with questions ranging in nature from a fear of commitment and intimacy, to *whom* and *how* it's OK to date, to the prevalence of online dating sites, to STDs and unplanned pregnancy, to the possibility of marriage. Remember, your job is not to be an expert in all things relating to intimacy. Your work is to come alongside students, and the questions they have, and look for the already present work of God in their lives.

THE MENTOR'S TOOLBOX

- What do you remember from your own relational journey toward intimacy? What do you remember about the different relational paradigms that were described above? Do you remember anything significant as it relates to transitioning from one paradigm to another?
- What were some of your own struggles with desiring and pursuing intimacy?
- What lessons did you learn about intimacy that you think *all* college students should be made aware of?
- We've all made mistakes when it comes to the pursuit of intimacy. Are there some that still haunt you to this day? If so, how can you surrender those to God once and for all?
- What is your biggest fear, or reservation, as it relates to talking with students in this area? No relationship is perfect, so how can students learn from you in regard to where you are at in your own pursuit of "healthy" relationships?

Take some time to reflect on these questions in the space provided on the following page.

Here are several questions that might help to promote conversation with your student in this area:
- Have you ever been in what you would call a "serious" relationship? If so, tell me about it. If not, why do you think that is? Do you want to be in a relationship? Why or why not?
- What has served to shape your understanding of relationships in general? How has your parents' relationship shaped your perspective? How have your friends? How have your friends' parents' relationships shaped you?
- How has media and pop culture shaped your understanding of relationships? Do you think relationships are portrayed accurately in the media? If so, how? If not, why not? Why might Hollywood misrepresent what relationships are really like?

~ continued on the next page

- What does the word "intimacy" mean to you? Does the idea of it scare you? Does it make you excited? Have you been intimate with others before? When is it (or in what ways is it) OK to be intimate with another?
- How would you describe a healthy relationship? Have you ever seen a relationship that you would describe as healthy? If so, by whom? What did their relationship look like? What characteristics would you hope to emulate in your own relationship someday?

For further reading on the subject of intimacy, consider:
- *Sex & the Soul* by Donna Freitas
- *Fit to Be Tied* by Bill and Lynne Hybels

Notes, questions, reminders,
points of action, etc.

11

"Others"

Fear » Fascination » Friend

The King will reply, "Truly I tell you,
whatever you did for one of the least of these
brothers and sisters of mine, you did for me."
— Matthew 25:40

Do nothing out of selfish ambition or vain conceit.
Rather, in humility value others above yourselves.
— Philippians 2:3

The college years are often marked by the exposure to new things. New people, new places, new ideas, and new experiences serve equally, alongside the prescribed curriculum, as a teaching tool for students. It is a place filled with highly-educated professors, classmates from varied backgrounds and ethnicities, and a context that is designed to educate, challenge, and grow students. The college experience is an optimal opportunity for students to be exposed to, and engage with, the "others." And as they do, they'll be challenged to reconsider the ways in which they may have been misguided in their thinking about others—someone of another race or religion, gender or sexual identity, political or economic background.

And it's not necessarily about changing anyone's views—although in some instances it might very well involve that—but more so about learning how to better relate to those people who are different, those people who were previously unknown.

Much of this ties back into the chapter talking about life lens (chap. 4). When students head off to college, they bring with them eighteen years of conditioning, having been taught how to view, interpret, and understand the world in which they live. Their life lens has been shaped by the adults in their world (parents, grandparents, pastors, professors, coaches, etc.) who have their own experiences and views about people of different races, religions, genders, sexual orientations, political parties, social classes, and so forth. In their own way(s), because of their own upbringing and personal experience, they instill in their young students certain ways of thinking that often aren't challenged until they arrive on campus and are exposed to something different. The world is indeed getting smaller as a result of all of the technological advances that allow us to connect with people from around the world, but a number of factors still keep us divided as a human race.

Many students will come to campus having been influenced by (their parents, pastors, or friends back home) one thing or another about "strangers." The perceived other is a relative unknown that our students have been taught to fear, hate, be suspicious of, look down upon, ignore, oppress, or discriminate against—be it intentional or not. The distinctions may fall along racial, denominational, political, religious, affinity, sexual identity, or some other barrier that a student has been told to avoid and/or taught to fear.

But the college context will put these familiar and ingrained ways of thinking and living to the test. Internally or externally, students will quickly find themselves in tension physically, emotionally, and mentally with others—and will be challenged to reconsider what they say they believe in regards to the other. This can be quite a strenuous, and even painful, process for students to go through.

The college environment typically provides a place for students to come face-to-face with some (or even all) of these perceived others. When they do, our students must be challenged to push beyond their initial fears, to become more open to these unknowns. While learning more about the other, and what they are *really* all about, students must be encouraged to go even further—from a curious openness to authentic and intentional relationships—such that the other becomes a friend.

Faith has too often served as a reason for separation, suspicion, and even fear. It must, however, become a catalyst to engage with, and better relate to, those who are different—not for the sake of conversation, or even conversion, but for the sake of loving thy neighbor. It is a part of our call to love God and love others, or love God by loving others.

And it should be noted that I'm talking about something wholly different from our culture's call to tolerance. As it is being played out in our American culture, tolerance is about stripping away those things that make us different—and therefore serving to divide us—such that we're boiled down to our collective least common denominator. It feels like a cooperative watering down of our cultural differences in order to bring about peace. And while the sentiment or motivation behind this call to tolerance may be worthy, it is unhelpful and unbiblical.

What I am suggesting, instead, is that we take the path of hospitality and charity with those who are different, or other. And while a lot could be said about hospitality and charity, for the sake of this conversation I'd like us to think about these terms in this way:

- *Hospitality* creates space for those who believe and live differently than we do.
- *Charity* confesses that we may not know everything, or be correct about everything, and is humble enough to admit that we just might have something to learn from someone who is different.

This isn't a call to deny or even change one's beliefs or practices but more a call to see the other as equally created in the image of God—and worthy of the same human dignities that we presume for ourselves. It also entails maintaining openness to any change that God may want to work in one's life as a result.

The college years are the ideal context for exposing young people to new and different experiences. It's an important time for acknowledging stereotypes and moving beyond them—for facing fears head on, for overcoming hang-ups and hostilities. A part of your work as a Mentor will be to encourage your students to identify, engage, and really get to know the unknown, the other. And while the context of the college years is ideal, students should be encouraged and/or challenged into this process in their own unique way.

Fear

I once had a student who came to campus from an extremely conservative background. The campus offered some educational opportunities that she was really excited about. But truth be told, she was quite nervous about what coming to campus could be like for her. She was firm in her beliefs and had very strong convictions about how a Christian should live. She wasn't afraid that she'd lose her faith, but she wondered whether its intensity could create tension for those who believed (and lived) different from her.

Well, she wasn't on campus for long before she started to experience some fairly high levels of tension, and it wasn't the kind of tension she had anticipated—more appropriately put, the source of her tension was not what she had anticipated. It wasn't that she was bumping up against people who were put off by her deep faith and clearly defined convictions but, more so, her own struggle to hold on to the same faith and convictions she had come to campus with, in light of some of the people she was encountering.

Her tension was internal.

She was struggling to see how the beliefs that she had long held, without question, now fit with her new—changing—reality. She had come from a relatively small town in the South, where she believed certain things about certain people—most of whom she had never had any real personal contact with, which made believing those things rather easy.

But now on campus, she was a part of a much more diverse community, coming face-to-face with assorted "others" who were not living up to the scary billing they had been given. She was struggling to believe the things that she was told and taught as a youth were indeed true. Even worse, these struggles she was having in a few areas were projecting themselves onto a multitude of other areas. In her mind, everything was being called into question, and she was struggling to know how to deal with it all.

It felt to her as if her world was crumbling.

> > >

Going off to college can be one of the most exciting times in a young person's life. There's so much potential, so much that's possible. Yet, at the same time, it can be an incredibly scary experience for a number of our students who don't have much exposure to those things and people different from them. Depending on the homes and communities that they come from, it's quite possible the new, diverse campus community is filled with much that has previously been defined to them as different, bad, or even evil.

Intentionally or not, many students have been taught to fear that which is different from them, and on most campuses students will encounter much that is different, which naturally sets the table for a kind of showdown—internal and/or external.

Whether instinctive or intentional, some students will begin to wall themselves off from the "others" around campus. They choose to stick to those who are just like them. They look on everyone else with a suspicious eye. They experience levels of fear whenever out, in uncontrolled contexts, fearful of what

"Other People" were listed at #4 on a list of the Top 10 Things People Fear Most.

Social phobia affects about 15 million American adults, according to the National Institute of Mental Health. And it's not limited to public speaking: Those affected can get the sweats over eating or drinking in front of others, or a general anxiety when around almost anyone other than family members. The fear begins in childhood or adolescence, usually around the age of 13.

— www.livescience.com[1]

they could be exposed to and believing that others might be out for them.

It may sound a bit extreme, but I've seen it. And you can't quickly undo eighteen years of thinking and living. The fears and feelings about others are deeply woven into the fabric of our young students. So it will likely take some time to begin to loosen some of those old ways of believing in order to move toward a more healthy way of living.

But with loosening comes another set of fears, causing some to wonder, *If I was wrong about "X," then what else might I be wrong about? What else might "they"* [their parents, pastors, etc.] *have taught me that was also wrong?* They fear that if they begin to pull on that exposed thread the entire garment they're wearing may begin to unravel before their very eyes. And this will leave them with little more than a messy pile of string and a mounting (albeit changing) set of fears. With so much else feeling out of their control in the college context, something as personal and central to their identity as their beliefs can be a scary thing to consider messing with.

So it doesn't often happen on purpose. Students seldom go out in search of the kinds of interactions and experiences that can serve to challenge them at their very core. Instead, it's more often the random encounters, the casual interactions, or even the forced engagement (because of a class assignment, room-mate situation, work shift, etc.), that slowly begins to open students to the possibility that they (and those who had previously taught them) might have been wrong in their beliefs. This will obviously, for reasons already mentioned, create a good deal of internal tension—and even resistance. But slowly, some students will begin to let their guard down and open themselves up to the idea of no longer fearing people who are different from them. And a part of your job as a Mentor is to encourage them in this direction.

Fascination

When is the last time you were part of an awkward getting-to-know-you-for-the-first-time kind of conversation?

Do you remember?

They can be painful. Everything is new and unfamiliar; boundaries are unknown. If you add to this any *known* differences (i.e., race, religion, denomination, gender, sexual identity, political preference, etc.), then the list of potential land mines goes up exponentially. While some people handle these scenarios quite well, others shouldn't be allowed to talk in (much less find their way into) situations like this because sensitivity is an important element when beginning to relate with people who are different.

Consider several awkward questions that might roll through one's mind and, depending on the level of sensitivity and ability to filter themselves, could potentially be voiced:

- You're not from around here, are you?
- Who are you?
- What do you call yourself?
- Why would you believe that?
- How much do you [or your family] make?
- Do you know that's sinful?
- Do you know your wrong about that?

These are a quick sampling of questions that *could* naturally come up in an exploratory conversation with someone new—and evidence of how a simple desire to get to know someone could easily begin to feel like a courtroom interrogation (imagine each of the questions above being thrown at the intended target in rapid-fire succession). It's not that the inquisitor is trying to make their new acquaintance feel uncomfortable. It is more an attempt to fill any awkward silence with honest (though maybe insensitive) questions that they'd like to know the answers to.

Much like a child who's in the developmental stage of taking in a multitude of new things, each and every day, and going to his parent(s) with question upon question (upon question upon question), there is a legitimate desire to learn. Some questions are better than others. Some questions are more appropriate than others (although a child would not be expected to know such boundaries as readily as someone much older). But the sincere inquisitive nature of the questioning stems from a desire to know more. To have answers. To become familiar.

> *Learning to see the so-called other as a friend increases our sensitivity to the reductionism, commodification and manipulation that plague some versions of mission and ministry. Human beings who are not Christians are far more than potential converts.*
>
> — Christopher L. Heuertz and Christine D. Pohl, *Friendship at the Margins*[2]

> > >

Often, all it takes is breaking the ice.

Once people are given the chance to face something (or someone) that was previously considered an unknown, and come to realize that they're really not all that different from them (and totally not "scary"), an interesting switch is often made: that which was once the source of fear suddenly becomes the focus of one's fascination. All of the silly taboos are exposed as untrue and unwarranted, which leaves the unknown rendered safe but still unknown. So one student, as if to make up for lost time, can begin to study her newfound friend as if she was on a dissection table.

The desire to learn is real, but the approach can be awkward, insensitive, or even offensive. It's not that a student means any harm by his or her line of questioning. In fact, it's typically quite the opposite. They're curious, and they haven't necessarily learned how to have these kinds of conversations because previously they were to avoid these others at all costs. They are different and likely haven't taken the time to consider how their differences might make early attempts and conversing more challenging than fruitful.

A part of the challenge lies in the fact that as the fascinated student embarks on the fact-finding expedition, it's done from a place of confidence (if not arrogance) in their own identity and beliefs. Yes, they're beginning to move away from this, but they're not there yet. So the kinds of questions they might be inclined to ask, and/or some of the assumptions they'll naturally make, will be rooted in a position of believing they're still in the right and their new friend, the wrong (or simply misguided). This phase of learning to relate to others can be marked by some level of charity but often still lacks any level of hospitality—not on purpose, of course, but simply out of a lack of experience.

This is a natural part of the progression from other toward friend, but in order for students to be able to get beyond this phase of "fascination," new levels of humility and sensitivity must be expressed. And the big challenge in this next step is not giving up one's own beliefs and practices (that are both healthy and appropriate), in order to make a friend.

Friend

This can be a difficult place to get to.

Achieving true friendship with someone who has long been considered a threat of some kind will necessitate a willingness to endure what can be a fairly lengthy and awkward phase in which a lot of questions are being asked and ideas are being shared. Misunderstandings are likely to abound. It requires both parties to be generous and gracious. It calls for increasing levels of charity and hospitality if friendship is to be achieved.

I recall a couple of college-aged friends, several years back now, who somehow found each other and were certain that they were going to help bring reconciliation to campus as it related to race relations. They believed this was an issue that needed to be addressed on campus in several intentional ways. After their first few visits to our office on campus, however, something happened, and their visits began to take on quite a different focus.

What had been focused on "them out there" suddenly turned onto their new, developing relationship. It may have been that they (temporarily) skipped the fascination phase of their relationship, but for the better part of the next two years these students were a regular fixture in our office. Some weeks were better than others; some weeks they came in smiling and in full embrace. Other weeks they seemed to come in begrudgingly, more out of obligation, and not all that fond of each other—but they still came of their own free will. They stuck with it. They journeyed through a lot of difficult (but interesting) questions and misunderstandings, and I think it helped (significantly) to have a third-party moderator of sorts involved (knowing that a pastor was sitting in on the conversation seemed to make the pointed line of questioning a little more palatable).

Eventually the conversations became a lot less tense and occurred with much greater frequency than their weekly visit to our office. The two became good friends, but it required a great deal of work. Both of them had to be consistent and committed to the process because it was just that: a process!

> > >

This is quite possibly one of the biggest and most significant transitions (or transformations) that can happen in a student's life. When the other becomes a true friend, something very special occurs. In many ways, it's a beautiful gift God has bestowed upon these individuals. They've been allowed to experience a piece of the kingdom of God, here on earth. That which once kept them divided has been exposed for the lie that it is, and a growing friendship is the result. It's the kind of thing that you wish each and all students could go through the first day they show up on campus, because this kind of paradigm shift has a way of opening students up to a multitude of possibilities in other areas of their lives.

>> *When community is working on all cylinders, the ripples of community touch the world.*
— Gabe Lyons, *The Next Christians*[3]

Friendship of this nature, like friendship of any kind, will take time. It cannot be forced. It cannot be rushed. It will slowly mature and develop as both parties come together with an openness and willingness to learn and grow and give to one another. Hospitality and charity. And in many ways, the idea of "other" can become obsolete in a students' changing reality. As their relationships change, they'll cease to see the differences that once kept them apart.

At least until they encounter someone who's still entrenched in an "other" mentality.

Sadly, those who don't understand this kind of broad-minded relationship are in our twenty-first-century America (and world); they don't like different. They prefer to keep to their own, and prefer it that everyone else do the same. Hate, for many, is still a common emotion toward people who are different, or believe different. And it's almost all fear based.

So a part of your work as Mentor is to encourage students on this journey of "other to friend," but an additional piece of your work with students needs to be helping them to understand the role they can play in continuing to break down the divisions that keep some divided.

They can be agents of hope.

Agents of education.

Agents of reconciliation.

People need to see that relationships with others are indeed possible. They need to see it lived out. They need to see sacrifice and compromise lived out. They need to see that people who are different—and who believe different things and live out different practices—can still be friends.

And it's important to reiterate here that this kind of friendship is one that allows both individuals to maintain their distinctive beliefs and practices (that are healthy and true, of course). Many students will be tempted to, in the name of friendship, relinquish *all* of those things that make friendship difficult, but that's not friendship. That's the kind of *cultural tolerance* mentioned early on in this chapter, and it doesn't show proper respect for the unique ways God has made us—or the unique journey He has us on. True friendship is able to humbly be confident in one's own beliefs and practice, while at the same time gracefully allowing another to hold to their own beliefs and practices. It's a friendship that doesn't demand or necessitate change—except where it's needed to correct stereotypes and misinformation. And while a lot could be said in regards to the opportunity to share one's faith within the context of this developing friendship, that is another conversation for another time (yet something your students may very well have questions about).

THE MENTOR'S TOOLBOX

- What were you taught growing up in regards to people who were "different" from you? Who taught you those things? What do you know about why they believed those things?
- What do you remember about your first encounter with someone who had been categorized as an "other"? What was it like? What was your initial feeling? Did anything happen during the initial encounter that served to reaffirm (or call into question) that which you had been previously told?
- Who are the people you still struggle to relate to? What makes it such a struggle? What can you do to help resolve this situation?
- What's a story you have about a once other becoming a friend? Do you have any funny (or awkward or embarrassing) stories to share from the "fascination" phase of your relationship?
- Do you think today's students have it easier or more difficult when it comes to addressing this area of other? Why? What's changed in our culture?

Take some time to reflect on these questions in the space provided on the following page.

Here are several questions that might help to promote conversation with your student in this area:

- Who are the "others" in your world? Who is it that you've been "warned" about? Are there certain kinds of people who your parents (or pastors, etc.) told you to avoid when arriving on campus?
- Are there people you fear? If so, why? Are those fears warranted? Why or why not? Where do you think those fears come from?
- Who have you met that surprised you because they were different than you expected them to be? What were some of the preconceived notions that you had about them? How were those notions proven wrong?

~ continued on the next page

- How have you gone about engaging people who are different from you? What has been the biggest challenge? Struggle? What has surprised you as you've engaged in this process?
- Talk about a new friend who was once categorized as an other in your mind. What happened? Talk about the journey from other to friend. Were there any stories that could fall in the awkward "fascination" phase of exploring a newfound friend?

For further reading on the subject of "Others," consider:
- *Friendship at the Margins* by Chris Heuertz and Christine Pohl
- *Making Room* by Christine Pohl

Notes, questions, reminders,
points of action, etc.

12
Mentors

Self-Guided » "Other" Guided » Co-Guided

Start children off on the way they should go,
and even when they are old they will not turn from it.
— Proverbs 22:6

Even when I am old and gray, do not forsake me, my God,
till I declare your power to the next generation,
your mighty acts to all who are to come.
— Psalm 71:18

Over the course of the past fifteen years I've observed a gradual trend *away* from mentoring relationships on campus.

Oh, I didn't mention that before?

I thought you knew.

OK, maybe my reasoning for saving this chapter until the very end of the book was somewhat strategic in nature. I know that the idea of putting yourself out there with college students probably seems daunting in and of itself, and I didn't want to add to your own reservations by telling you that this process has become much more of a challenge over the course of the past decade in particular.

No, not all mentoring relationships have gone away. There are still students who are seeking the kind of meaningful relationships that can be found with men and women who have lived a bit more life, and might just have something meaningful to share with this up-and-coming generation. But the number of students who are *pursuing* these kinds of relationships is rapidly in decline.

Part of this is our fault as Mentors because we've taken a passive posture of sitting back and waiting for students to pursue us. We assume that if they want to be mentored they will seek us out and initiate that kind of relationship. We rationalize that most students are so busy that we'd rather not add to their already full plate by extending them an invitation to quite an intentional and involved relationship. If we're honest, we fear (maybe just a little) sticking our neck out, not knowing if a student will really be interested in this kind of experience anyway. We make the assumption that students know where (and how) to find us, when (or if) they're ready for this kind of thing.

But we can't sit back and wait.

We need to be better about initiating these kinds of formative relationships.

We need to do our part, and we need to be willing to let students do their part.

And what is the student's part? Well, it might very well be to initiate this kind of relationship, but most of them look at us and figure that we're too busy, and that they probably shouldn't bother asking. For others it will be to accept our invitation into relationship, but many students will need to jump a couple of sizeable hurdles before they can see their way clear to do this.

The first hurdle is this: a lack of trust in authority, one of the signatures of postmodernism. Students have grown suspicious of anyone claiming to be an expert, or holding the kind of power that can shape and/or control environments and people. We can't fault them for this, however, because we've all seen the scandals reported in the news, revealing the abuse of power and authority for personal gain or pleasure. These individuals (or organizations) had asked people to trust them then misused that trust. And our youth, rather than try to distinguish the good from the bad, have decided it is easier to lump all power mongers into one untrustworthy group. The well-intended Mentor is unfortunately included in this untrustworthy mishmash.

The second major hurdle is: a desire to let experience be the guide, another signature of postmodernism. Young men and women believe that personal experience is the best educator, especially in light of the aforementioned issues with authority figures and experts. They would rather experience life for themselves, without the assistance of any sort of guide. And they believe that, regardless of the nature of the experience—good or bad—the *self*-education will ultimately be worth it. As you can imagine, this puts our students in vulnerable positions, and increases the likelihood that they'll spend their formative college years wandering aimlessly about or finding their way into numerous messes that could have been avoided.

As Mentors we cannot sit idly by and allow our students to waste this significant season of life. College is a once-in-a-lifetime experience that requires their intentional attention to the areas that I've already discussed in this book. They have unique exposure and access to well-educated and highly experienced individuals (like you), and the potential these years hold within them is too significant to be squandered by a generation unwilling to see the value of mentoring relationships. The college years are filled with a number of life-shaping decisions, most of which Mentors have likely journeyed through themselves, and this makes going about these years without the helpful assistance a mentor can provide seem crazy.

With the wealth of mentoring resources often found on or near college campuses—or through the conveniences provided by technological advances—students need to be willing to *prioritize* time with someone who is older, wiser, and interested in investing in them. There are so many ways that a mentoring relationship can, and should, benefit college students—and not just during the college years but well beyond.

Some students will awaken to this need, and given their all or nothing nature, may do a 180 and choose to give the keys to their lives to their Mentors. From doing it all themselves to simply wanting to have it done for them, many students will struggle to understand how to enter into a mentoring relationship. In some ways it will seem easier to simply take those keys and begin to map out a productive route for students to take over the course of their remaining time on campus. While that might benefit them in the short term, it does not assist them in the ways that a good, healthy mentoring relationship does.

The real key for your student(s) will be in finding a balance between taking on increasing levels of responsibility for their own lives, while at the same time maintaining openness to the suggestions of a trusted mentor in their lives, which we hope will ultimately yield growth and maturation in how to think, believe, and live well in the world.

But let's start back at the beginning.

Self-Guided

Approximately one hundred student-led clubs and organizations are on the campus I currently serve. Of that number, eight to twelve (depending on the semester) are categorized as Faith Development Organizations. These groups, although registered through Student Affairs—like all other clubs and organizations on campus—have a special relationship with the Office of University Ministries.

Each group is student led and student initiated and (theoretically) represents differing denominational or affinity orientations. While a couple of these groups are more clearly distinguishable from the rest, because of who they represent and how they function, the majority of them could pretty easily be mistaken for one another. They *look* the same, *sound* the same, and *function* more or less the same. The only thing that's different, aside from their name, is who's in charge.

And so they go, ebbing and flowing on the ability and charisma of the student leaders, to draw (and keep) a crowd of students who will allow them to do their thing. To lead a ministry according to how *they* feel led or see fit.

Of course, they're not left out there on their own, without any assistance or advisement at all. Each of these groups is required to have a staff or faculty advisor, but for most groups this is simply an obligatory position. A signature. A safety net. Still, the group is theirs! Come hell or high water, the group is theirs to do with as they please. And not surprisingly, from one year to the next we indeed see these groups rise and fall based on the passion and capabilities of the student leaders. What is wildly popular (and meaningful) one year could cease to exist the following year because of poor foresight on the part of the student leaders. Whether it's something as trivial as forgetting to file the paperwork on time or something more substantial like neglecting to prepare and equip a crop of leaders to step into any leadership vacancies, much of the ministry's stability is placed in the hands of a few eager students. And in our current campus (and cultural) climate, they wouldn't have it any other way. If it's going to fail or flop, it's going to do so because of *students'* decisions—and no one else's.

This is only one example among many. Today's students want the freedom to create and control, no matter what the results.

> > >

Today's students are leaders. . . .

OK, well, maybe not all of them. The vast majority of them, however, are claiming a certain level of ownership and responsibility for their lives (albeit by default) by choosing to forego the kind of fruitful growth that can come from a mentoring relationship. They're not interested in doing it your way. They want to live life on their own terms. They want to experience all that life has to offer.

They want to be free.

They want to create.

They want to control.

And they don't want you and your wisdom about right and wrong, true or false, this or that getting in their way.

Increasingly, whenever possible, students are opting out of those environments and situations in which they feel bound. Things that feel overly institutionalized, traditional, or even too adult led, have lost much of their appeal to today's students. Many of them want you to believe that if you (as an adult) will simply get out of the way and let them do it their way, then it will be perfect. No matter what *it* is.

In similar fashion, more and more students today are stepping out as creators. They've been raised in the Age of the Internet— where anyone with a great idea and a little know-how can make millions (or even billions). They've got an entrepreneurial spirit that courses through their veins and beckons them toward blank canvases. They don't like being tied down by other people's ideas. They feel the need to be freed up to create yet supported in their creative endeavors because, well, they don't have any money or "power." They do, however, have creativity.

The desire to create is not a bad thing at all! In fact, it speaks to being created in the image of the Creator. Still, for many of today's students, the space to create trumps all, and it ultimately comes down to control. They distrust the power holders (unless they're students—one of their own). They want to experience things for themselves, and they're increasingly inclined to opt out of those things that do not fit to this form.

This tends to limit our response to (and opportunity with) these students. We either yield to their desires, relinquishing our control as leaders and Mentors—and have hope that an opportunity to speak into their life eventually presents itself (and they're open to it)—*or* we attempt to reset the table and let them know that they're in our world and need to play by our rules. This is incredibly risky because if students opt out they may opt out for good, and we'll miss out on any future opportunities to speak into their lives.

Strangely, after talking throughout this book about students operating out of a black or white mind-set, that, as Mentors, we find ourselves cornered.

> *The desire for autonomy is a symptom of a season that occurs naturally in nearly everyone's life. Unfortunately, some get this autonomy too soon, whereas some don't get it at all. Many kids sneak by their parents or teachers and steal autonomy early. They think they're ready, but often aren't— and accidents happen.*
> — Tim Elmore, *Artificial Maturity*[1]

And yet, I believe that if we are able to give just enough to students—just enough of the creative control and decision-making authority—without giving away the farm, we'll earn ourselves the right to (eventually) be heard.

Other-Guided

I once met weekly with a student for an entire semester. When we got together, he shared with me about a specific struggle he was dealing with, and week after week it was as if we were having the same conversation.

His complaint was always the same.

He never seemed to see any progress in his life.

He felt stuck.

Once a week, after he lamented his very real struggle, we prayed and brainstormed possible solutions to managing his struggle. Often those solutions took on similar form: define several practical steps that he could take, describe the kind of people he could invite to serve as layers of accountability, and outline the role I was willing to play in this process—and always the role that God and God alone could and should play.

But week after week, when I'd ask about how his work was going, and whether he had set into motion the accountable relationships that we had talked about, he always had excuses. Then he'd question God's inactivity and wonder why things weren't changing. And although he never verbally questioned my role in this process, there seemed to be an underlying, unexpressed expectation that I was going to take care of this for him (and a growing frustration because I was not).

We met for an entire semester—fifteen *long* weeks—and by the end, I think we had both given up on the process.

He had come to me wanting my pastoral assistance, But for him, the unspoken expectation was that I would fix him and he would no longer struggle in this area. He was unwilling to do the kind of hard work that only *he* could do, and he was unwilling to invite any one of his peers into the process.

He was willing to acknowledge the problem, and the need to deal with it, but wanted someone else to do all of the heavy lifting. I wasn't willing to do that for him. It wasn't my job. It was his.

> > >

We have made it an illness to show weakness in much of our Christian culture. Although we would never confess it, an unspoken expectation exists that people are supposed to have it all together in our communities of faith. Or at least that's the perception that a lot of Christians have of churches, small groups, and other Christian communities. This causes many Christians to attempt to do life solo. They feel the need to clean up their act *before* they would consider themselves worthy of joining the fellowship of other Christians.

Many Christians will struggle with this line of thinking until there's a breakthrough of some kind, at which point many (young and old) feel as if they're suddenly not in it alone. They will see the Christian community for the support structure it can be and are so weary of fighting alone that they collapse into the fellowship's embrace. And because of their mental, emotional, and spiritual exhaustion, they often put themselves in a position to receive—to quite literally be poured into.

> *Mentoring has a trajectory, an aim, a target and a purpose. It is not mindless or soulless meandering but a journey that recognizes itself as pilgrimage, a journey of spiritual and devotional purpose. The trajectory is purposive but not prepackaged.*
>
> — Keith Anderson and Randy Reese, *Spiritual Mentoring*[2]

They've figured out that they don't have what it takes, so it's time to glean from someone who is older and wiser. It becomes something more than a healthy gleaning from a Mentor and often looks more like a regression to an early developmental stage in which they did what they were told, and mimicked what they saw being done. It was a stage that lacked any critical thought or personal decision making.

While this was completely acceptable (and developmentally appropriate) as toddlers and preschoolers, it is not at the college level. As Mentors, our role is not to give our students all the answers but to help them ask better questions. How to discern truth from fiction. How to begin to better think (and act) like a responsible adult.

Co-Guided

I graduated from college in 1997, and my college years were a time of incredible growth and formation, in part, because of one of my campus pastors—Keith. We spent a lot of time together over the course of my sophomore, junior, and senior years. He invested heavily in me, and I doubt I'd be the person I am, or be in the position I am in, without our time together.

And we've stayed connected to this very day.

The relationship Keith and I have has changed since its inception in large part because of the multiple relocations that have us hundreds of miles apart. But it has also changed because, at some point along the way (unknown to me), Keith allowed me to speak into his life. As a Mentor, he didn't need to do this. I never made this request. I never demanded to be heard. In fact, I'm sure that once I finally picked up on what he was doing, I tried to shut it down, believing that I had nothing to offer this incredible man of God.

Yet that wasn't how Keith saw it.

He believed, increasingly so, that I had something to offer during our times together. It was both humbling and uplifting. His self-sacrifice of power and authority within our relationship paved the way for greater growth and formation in my own life, as well as a maturation of our relationship—and he continues to be a Mentor (and friend) of mine.

Keith offered incredible insight and wisdom sometimes through what he said and sometimes through what he left unsaid. Often, his wisdom and insight came in the form of a question that caused me to have to engage—with my head and my heart—in ways that shaped me.

He wasn't only feeding me but teaching me how to feed myself.

And this is the goal of our work with students . . . right?!

> > >

As we walk with our students, talking with them and encouraging them along the way, we are helping them to grow up in many intentional ways during one of the most formative seasons of their life.

As a Mentor, it *cannot* be about us. It cannot be about making college-aged replications of ourselves. This is an incredible task and is all—*ALL*—about the success of our young friends. The members of this up-and-coming generation are the future leaders of our world.

Our task, from the very beginning, has been to help them to take responsibility for their own lives—and to increasingly see themselves as implicated in the world, such that they offer themselves up as God's agents to be used as *He* desires, no matter the context.

And until this chapter, you were probably under the assumption that this wasn't going to be all that difficult.

Sorry about that.

I believe with all of my heart that if we can get students to recognize their need for the kind of mentoring relationship that we're availing ourselves to, and then their need to stay invested in their own ongoing growth and development, we actually set the table for quite a special relationship—the kind of relationship with the potential to be both life giving and transformative for both parties involved.

> *The mentoree plays an active and involved role in the process of mentoring. . . . Mentoring is a mutual process actively involving both mentor and mentoree.*
>
> — Anderson and Reese, *Spiritual Mentoring*[3]

I'm so grateful for all of the souls who have invested in me over the course of my life. Starting long before I was a Christian and stretching all the way up to this day, I am the product of a lot (*a lot!*) of other people's selfless giving.

And I'm equally grateful for the students who have allowed me to journey with them over the course of the past fifteen years, spanning four different campuses. They've taught me much about what it means to be a Mentor. They've helped me to rework my approaches and refine my strategies, and to recognize the God's ever-present work in our midst.

Mentors are special people.

Truthfully, we have the potential to shape the world—one life at a time.

THE MENTOR'S TOOLBOX

- Who have been the most significant mentors in your life? Why? What made them so special?
- What is one of the greatest lessons a mentor taught you (or helped you to realize)? How has that lesson served to shape you all these many years later?
- Do you have a mentor now? Is there someone who consistently pours into your life—regardless of your age and/or position in life? If not, why not? If so, what's behind your decision to continue this kind of relationship?
- Who are you serving as a mentor for? What does it look like? How intentional are you being in your approach? Would the other person refer to you as a "mentor"? If not, why not? Are there ways you might need to up your level of intentionality?

Take some time to reflect on these questions in the space provided on the following page.

Here are several questions that might help to promote conversation with your student in this area:
- How do you navigate life? Who helps you to make decisions? Who do you talk with about the things you don't understand? Is there someone you spend time with whose sole interest is you and your success?
- Have you ever had a mentor that you can think of? Who was it? What did that relationship look like? What did you learn from it? How did it shape you? How did it end?
- Do you value the insight and experience of others? Are you the kind of person who is willing to learn from others? Would you consider yourself teachable? If not, why not?
- Have you ever had an intentional relationship with someone you would consider "older and wiser"? If so, how did that come to be? Who initiated it? What was the point of the relationship? Are you still connected? How significant would you say that relationship was for you? Why?

~ continued on the next page

THE MENTOR'S TOOLBOX

- Do you believe you have anything to offer those you would classify as "older and wiser"? If so, what is it? Are there ways in which you're having a chance to share that? If not, why not? What would a "mutually beneficial" mentoring relationship look like to you?
- Can you see how a mentoring relationship could benefit you and your future? If so, how? If not, why do you think that is?

For further reading on the subject of mentoring, consider:
- *Spiritual Mentoring* by Keith Anderson and Randy Reese
- *Artificial Maturity* by Tim Elmore

Notes, questions, reminders,
points of action, etc.

Final Words

Why Does It Matter »
and What Does It All Mean?

Well, here we are.

We've arrived at the end of the book, the place where I tie it all together and put a pretty bow on the top. This is a neat little prepackaged experience for you to use with your student(s) to help them make the most of their formative college years.

Right?

Wrong.

This is where I point you back to the opening chapter in which I talked about how we would look at a number of different areas where students must be challenged to think about, to make some decisions, and begin to live out. I also mentioned that there is no one-size-fits-all approach to walking with college students.

Students are all different.

As are Mentors.

So you'll need to feel your way into this—and through it—in ways that seem best to you, especially as it relates to the individual students you may walk with. I have chosen to be descriptive versus prescriptive throughout this work. I've *described* the kinds of conversations that must occur and the ways that students need to be challenged to step into new levels of responsibility in a wide variety of ways during their college years. I did not attempt to *prescribe* one particular approach to this because that would have been foolish.

What lies before you is an opportunity to prayerfully enter into an intentional relationship with a student—or number of students—where God has long been at work. You'll start by helping your students to see (and understand) God's present activity within them while then together considering some important areas where God desires to work through the student as they further grow and develop.

Depending on the student, some areas will need more focused time and attention than others. Some students will struggle more than others to work through specific areas, such as letting God into parts of their lives. And some students will struggle more than others to let *you*—as the Mentor—into certain areas of their lives.

Why Does It Matter?

It matters because college students matter.

They matter to God, and they should matter to you too.

While most college students love to believe they will be "complete" come graduation day, not lacking in any area, we know this won't be true. The reality is, they will have just begun what hopefully is a lifelong process of growth and formation.

While the university context is designed to serve as a catalyst for asking tough questions, pursuing truth, gaining experience, stepping into responsibility, and growing in a variety of ways, graduation will not be the end of the process. This kind of work requires the intentional participation of each and every student— for him or herself and, ultimately, for others—long after they graduate. It also necessitates a willingness to invite God into the process, into the very center of this process.

And this won't just happen. It will require intentional choices and priorities on the part of students.

As the students' engage their abilities in these different areas, with God, they will begin to invest in their own formation, and will set a trajectory for their lives long after their graduation. For those who choose to fully utilize their highly formative college years as a time to begin the transition process, growth, maturation, spiritual formation, and transformation will result.

But for those students who *don't* take advantage of this fertile season of life and, instead, allow themselves to become *victims* of the muck and mire of emerging adulthood, life (in many ways) will be put on hold or, worse yet, permanently stunted.

In many ways it is the tale of two students—much like it always has been.

Some find their paths into the fortunate and formative relationships that prove to be life giving and life shaping in ways they never would have dreamed possible. Their hearts and minds are opened up to new and formative things within the context of a safe relationship that leads to growth and further opportunity.

Other students, however, will never find (or simply choose to forego) this kind of relationship and will waste most (if not all) of their formative college years simply wandering about—acting as if they were still in high school and struggling to see how the college experiences offered them anything more than a slip of paper.

While these two types of students come to us in relatively similar places, they stand a great distance apart by the time they graduate. One much more prepared and equipped for the future. One much more confident in whom they are (becoming) and open to God's leading in their lives. One much more aware of the significance of different relationships, and how to go about engaging in them. One seemingly having a leg up on the other.

Remember, both types have their degrees, but their time on campus has been drastically different.

What Does It All Mean?

The long and short of it? *You matter.*

You are the X-factor in someone's college experience, in their journey through some of the most formative years of their lives.

You have the chance to make a difference. To be a game-changer. To help students (better) transition from youth to adulthood.

The university will continue to be a place of education, information, and preparation. God will continue to pursue this up-and-coming generation, watching and waiting for the opportunity to join with them in the process of becoming all that He is creating them to be.

But they need help getting out of their own way.

And they need help finding their way.

That's why they need *you*!

Will you come alongside college students and work with God to awaken them to the incredible potential that lies within this formative season of life?

Will you follow God's lead and help students to do the same?

Will you challenge and encourage your student(s) to step into the responsibility and embrace the transition that God wants to accomplish in them during these college years?

Most students will not find their way on their own.

Students need a guide.

Students need *you*!

And you are not alone, so allow me to invite you over to http://faithoncampus.com to continue this conversation—and to further provide resources for your important work as a Mentor to college students.

The need has never been so evident, and God's been preparing *you* to serve in this capacity for all of your life. Seize the day and become a Mentor to a young person on his or her journey toward a mature life in Christ.

I promise you won't regret it!

THE MENTOR'S TOOLBOX

- Do you believe today's college students need help finding their way?
- Do you believe that you can make a difference in the life of a young person?
- Who is the student (or, who are the students) who you need to be more intentional with? Who are the students who are ready for this kind of intentional relationship?
- In what ways are you feeling encouraged and better equipped for this journey? In what ways do you still feel inadequate? How might you surrender those feelings of inadequacy to God, such that His power is made perfect in your weakness?

Take some time to reflect on these questions in the space provided on the following page.

Notes, questions, reminders,
points of action, etc.

Notes

Chapter 1

1. Dr. Jeffrey Arnett, *Emerging Adulthood: The Winding Road from Late Teens through the Twenties* (New York: 2004, Oxford University Press), 8.

Chapter 2

1. Keith R. Anderson and Randy D. Reese, *Spiritual Mentoring: A Guide for Seeking and Giving Direction* (Downers Grove, IL: InterVarsity Press, 1999), 21.

2. Ibid., 102.

3. Ibid., 45.

Chapter 3.1

1. David Kinnaman, *You Lost Me: Why Young Christians Are Leaving Church . . . And Rethinking Faith* (Grand Rapids: Baker Books), 23.

2. Accessed October 9, 2012, http://www.pewforum.org/Unaffiliated/nones-on-the-rise.aspx.

3. M. Robert Mulholland, *Invitation to a Journey* (Downers Grove, IL: InterVarsity Press, 1993), 12.

Chapter 3.2

1. George Barna, "Most Twentysomethings Put Christianity on the Shelf Following Spiritually Active Teen Years." Online article: http://www.barna.org/barna-update/article/16-teensnext-gen/147-most-twentysomethings-put-christianity-on-the-shelf-following-spiritually-active-teen-years.

2. Thomas Merton, *Contemplative Prayer* (New York: Random House, 1996), 37.

3. Richard Foster, *Celebration of Discipline: The Path to Spiritual Growth* (New York: HarperCollins, 1998), 8.

4. M. Robert Mulholland, *Invitation to a Journey* (Downers Grove, IL: InterVarsity Press, 1993), 24.

Chapter 4

1. Keith Drury, paper presented, Fall Religion Colloquium, Indiana Wesleyan University, accessed October 30, 2012, http://www.drurywriting.com/keith/worldview.Christian.htm.

2. Accessed October 30, 2012, http://www.gallup.com/poll/148427/say-bible-literally.aspx.

3. David Kinnaman, *UnChristian* (Grand Rapids: Baker Books, 2007), 75.

4. Karl Barth, *Time* magazine, May 31, 1963, http://www.time.com/time/magazine/article/0,9171,896838,00.html.

Chapter 5

1. Accessed October 10, 2012, http://www.huffingtonpost.com/maura-kastberg/is-college-really-worth-i_b_1601192.html.

2. Accessed January 3, 2013, http://www.nytimes.com/2011/07/24/education/edlife/edl-24masters-t.html?pagewanted=all&_r=0.

3. Richard Arum and Josipa Roksa, *Academically Adrift: Limited Learning on College Campuses* (Chicago: The University of Chicago Press, 2011), 3.

4. Holly Epstein Ojalva, *Why Go To College At All?*, accessed October 30, 2012, http://thechoice.blogs.nytimes.com/2012/02/02/why-go-to-college-at-all/.

5. Steven Garber, *Fabric of Faithfulness: Weaving Together Belief and Behavior during the University Years* (Downers Grove, IL: InterVarsity Press, 2007), 43.

Chapter 6

1. Daniel Bortz, *How to Wean Your Children Off Your Expense Account*, accessed October 30, 2012, http://money.usnews.com/money/personal-finance/articles/2012/06/25/how-to-wean-your-children-off-your-expense-account.

2. *Parent Tips: Teaching Your College Student Financial Responsibility*, accessed October 31, 2012, http://www.business.ku.edu/news/releases/20081009-parent-tips-teaching-your-college-student-financial-responsibility.shtml.

3. Ibid.

Chapter 7

1. Karyl McBride, Ph.D., *Narcissism and Entitlement: "Do I Really Have to Stand in Line?,"* accessed October 31, 2012, http://www.psychologytoday.com/blog/the-legacy-distorted-love/201108/narcissism-and-entitlement-do-i-have-stand-in-line.

2. Elayne Clift, *From Students, a Misplaced Sense of Entitlement*, accessed October 31, 2012, http://chronicle.com/article/Students-Should-Check-Their/126890/.

3. Scot McKnight, *One.Life* (Grand Rapids: Zondervan, 2010), 154.

4. Frederick Buechner, *Wishful Thinking: A Theological ABC* (Harper & Row, 1973), 95.

Chapter 8

1. Wendell Berry, *Standing by Words: Essays* (Berkeley, CA: Counterpoint, 2011).

Chapter 9

1. Tim Elmore, *Generation iY: Our Last Chance to Save Them* (Atlanta: Poet Gardener Publishing, 2010), 39.

2. Accessed October 31, 2012, http://education-portal.com/articles/How_to_Develop_Lifelong_Friendships_while_in_College.html.

Chapter 10

1. Dick Purnell, accessed January 4, 2013, www.everystudent.com/features/search.html.

2. Tim Clydesdale, *The First Year Out* (Chicago: The University of Chicago Press, 2007), 83.

Chapter 11

1. Accessed January 4, 2013, http://www.livescience.com/13434-phobias-fears-acrophobia-heights-agoraphobia-arachnophobia.html.

2. Christopher L. Heuertz and Christine D. Pohl, *Friendship at the Margins: Discovering Mutuality in Service and Mission* (Downers Grove, IL: InterVarsity Press, 2010), 30.

3. Gabe Lyons, *The Next Christians: Seven Ways You Can Live the Gospel and Restore the World* (Colorado Springs: Multnomah Books, 2010), 156.

Chapter 12

1. Tim Elmore, *Artificial Maturity: Helping Kids Meet the Challenge of Becoming Authentic Adults* (San Francisco: Jossey-Bass, 2012), 56.

2. Keith R. Anderson and Randy D. Reese, *Spiritual Mentoring: A Guide for Seeking and Giving Direction* (Downers Grove, IL: InterVarsity Press, 1999), 48.

3. Ibid., 100.

About the Author

Dr. Guy Chmieleski serves as the university minister at Belmont University in Nashville, Tennessee. He is also the founder and primary author of *FaithONCampus.com*, a popular blog focused on better equipping mentors of college students.

Going off to college as a relatively new Christian, Guy experienced firsthand the power of mentoring relationships. In fact, it was one of Guy's campus pastors that first recognized in him a possible call to minister to college students.

Since graduating from Bethel University in 1997, Guy has gone on to serve students on campuses in southern Florida, Kentucky, and southern California before landing in Nashville in 2005. He has earned an MA in ministry from Palm Beach Atlantic University (2000) and a doctorate of ministry with an emphasis in spiritual formation and leadership development from George Fox Evangelical Seminary (2005).

Guy and his wife Heather reside just south of Nashville with their five children Derek, Autumn, Kaiya, Noll, and Lailie Grace.

You can connect with Guy on his blog: *FaithONCampus.com*. You can also find him on Twitter: @guychmieleski.